"Vacation Rental Success is a no-nor................................es
and even for the most seasoned home renter. Joel's knowledge as.............er,
owner and community activist—and his thirst for life as a world traveler—
come together in a highly engaging read."

– Lisa Pearson, Chief Marketing Officer Bazaarvoice

"This volume is packed with advice from some of the smartest people in
our industry. Joel is a seasoned guide who is ready and willing to show you
the way."

– Brian Sharples, CEO and Co-founder of HomeAway

"Joel's book gets right to the heart of what every new owner wants to know
– what are the most effective and efficient strategies for successfully owning
and managing a vacation rental, and how can I implement them quickly?
Vacation Rental Success is practical, straightforward, and filled with easy-to-
follow advice focused on taking action."

– John Banczak, former HomeAway Vice President and
Co-founder of TurnKey Vacation Rentals

"Vacation Rental Success is a Gold Mine! It's full of sage advice and trade secrets
for owners to avoid costly mistakes. Easy to read and easy to understand –
readers will reap the benefits of Joel's profitable instructions."

– Bob Easter, Author of Home Buying Power

"Joel's easy, conversation style belies the deep insights and years of experience
condensed into this practical and actionable guide. As a frequent customer of
vacation rentals, I had never considered turning my property into one – until
now! This is a must read for anyone interested in the vacation rental business."

– Jehmu Greene, Fox Business News Commentator

VACATION RENTAL SUCCESS

by Joel Rasmussen

Vacation Rental Success

by Joel Rasmussen

Mango Media, Inc.

DEDICATION

To my smart, sexy, funny partner of the last 20 years —
and to the amazing little man who lights up our life.

FORWARD

My love affair for vacation rentals began much as you'll discover Joel's did — with unforgettable family vacations. From the first time my family stayed in a vacation rental we were hooked, and have since experienced unique vacation rentals at the beach, on the slopes, and in cool cultural spots all over the world. However, I always found the process of booking vacation rentals online frustrating — I had to visit many different sites to be assured I had seen enough homes to feel confident I had found the perfect home for any given vacation. From this frustration, I had the idea to create HomeAway, a one-stop shop for renting these great homes.

I came to know Joel Rasmussen as he worked alongside our team at HomeAway to champion fair vacation rental regulations and individual property rights in Austin, the home of HomeAway's world headquarters. His ability to organize folks impressed me. His sincere and charismatic public speaking produced positive results with respect to Austin's short-term rental legislation.

Within these pages, Joel's love affair with vacation rentals will become clear to you, too. Vacation rentals have changed his life for the better, just as they've changed mine. I can tell you that as a vacation rental owner myself, his passion is so infectious that you can't help but get excited for the opportunities this book will present you. Joel explains what you need to know to get started the right way. But don't expect fluff; something I have learned about Joel is he gets straight to the point. And his "Vacation Rental Success Series" is packed with the nuts and bolts for setting up a successful vacation rental business, with advice from some of the smartest people in our industry.

Joel wants you to feel his dedication to introducing travelers to this special way of experiencing a place and time. More importantly, he wants you to learn about the many ways that a vacation rental business can expand your horizons. When you're ready to take action, Joel is a seasoned guide who is ready and willing to show you the way.

Brian Sharples
CEO and Co-founder of HomeAway, Inc.

TABLE OF CONTENTS

CHAPTER 4

CHAPTER 5

CHAPTER 6

CHAPTER 7

Security issues… Maintenance schedules… Which supplies do I need?

CHAPTER 8

Management steps… Handling staff and guests… Where can I find help?

PREFACE

What if you could fit a vacation into every work week? You could meet new and interesting people and share the local attractions with them… enjoy a beautiful and relaxing space… exchange nine to five (or six or seven) for a more flexible schedule. That's what I did — by renting out vacation property. Through hosting others, I gain the benefits of *their* time off, their exploration of a new place filled with the things that I love. I relish my "work," and I make enough profit to get away with my family a few times a year, always staying at a unique rental home run by someone with the same dreams as ours.

Interested? I'll show you how to determine if owning a vacation rental is for you, and whether you can make a go of it in your area. Are you a seasoned veteran who already has a property up and running? You'll discover great tips and tricks to find out how other proprietors have found success. Perhaps you're just curious about this lodging option for when you travel. This book has insights for you too.

Whether you've considered turning a second home into a vacation getaway or whether I have nudged you in that direction just now, you need to read this book, which spells out the ifs, ands, and buts of going into business for yourself. Owners who are knee-deep in the early stages of the vacation rental adventure can use this material as a prelude to the more advanced concepts of property management that I discuss in Volume Two of this series. Everyone can learn from my ups and downs, as well as from the advice and observations of the industry insiders that I present here — the big guns at the listing websites and in home security, advertising, and business administration.

Vacation Rental Success is for every reader who believes that life should be a holiday. If you've never left hotels behind for a stay in a vacation home, you'll be eager to do so when you find out why vacation rentals are superior lodging on every level. If you've always wanted to make a living that allows you to travel far and wide, you will learn that it is possible, and easier than you might think. I'll show you how to avoid the roadblocks and detours that stand between you and this thoroughly rewarding lifestyle. The door is open… come on in!

ACKNOWLEDGEMENTS

I am forever indebted to all of the folks in the Austin Rental Alliance who fought in the trenches with me, including Bob Easter, Kerry & Carol Price, Rachel Nation, Jay Reynolds, Cindy Hill, Sue Long, Peach & Cynthia Reynolds, Lauren Bard, Greg & Amanda Cribbs, Sandy Bowman, Lliana Mills, Todd & Amy Brand, BJ Heinley, Chereen Fischer; and to a number of great folks over at HomeAway, including: Victor Wang, Eileen Buesing, Matthew Curtis, Adam Annen, and Co-founders Brian Sharples and Carl Shepherd. I also wish to thank the strategic team who helped the ARA in Austin: Nikelle Mead, Mike Blizzard, and Mark Littlefield. And no acknowledgement would be complete without throwing heaps of praise on my editor, Nancy Osa. You are a magic worker!

Introduction

Tell me… what's your fondest travel memory? Was it seeing colors and patterns in a natural landscape unlike anything you'd ever seen before? Was it learning a new skill, like scuba diving, horseback riding, or how to make an ethereal soufflé? Perhaps it was a chance meeting with a local, a charismatic personality who has haunted your thoughts from time to time, ever since. Odds are, your most vivid memory is not checking into or checking out of yet another hotel, rushing through a cardboard continental breakfast, or avoiding eye contact when you pass the loud guests from room 216. It was probably the place you were visiting that made that space noteworthy—and not the other way around.

No wonder there is a growing interest in staying in unique short-term rental properties instead of hotels when people travel for business or fun, or when they're displaced from their houses during remodels or repairs. This new brand of traveler is hosted by individuals—often the owners themselves—not by corporations or their employees. And just who is doing the hosting these days? Anyone and everyone with a passion for the type of authentic experience that comes from staying in a private residence, near or far from home. I'll let you in on a little-known secret: Owning or renting vacation properties can be as satisfying for the host as it is for the guest. By putting yourself in your guests' shoes, you can deliver that special something that turns a vacation stay into a lifelong memory.

Joel Rasmussen

Think about it: When you drop your bags in a hotel, there's a feeling that you're somehow separate from life outside those walls — that you're sequestered from what's really happening on the streets. You can "go out" and witness local life, but you must eventually return to the isolation of your hotel. When you want solitude, you have to face guests in the hallway and staff in the lobby. A ride in the elevator stands between you and the pool. By contrast, when living in a private home, even just for a day or two, there is no separation. You engage in the energy of the area and carry that culture with you. You don't have to interact with "strangers." The people that you meet become genuine acquaintances and friends.

If this is how you prefer to travel when you venture to new places — and how you believe that others should experience travel — then chances are you would love owning or managing vacation rental properties. But isn't it risky trying to juggle a second home, pay taxes, and make the place pay for itself? Probably not as risky as you think.

What I've found firsthand is that vacation rentals change the math of real estate ownership. Not only can you afford a second abode that you can enjoy whenever you like, running this type of business holds the possibility of financial freedom. It can lead to increasing opportunities that you might not have realized are within your reach, eventually letting you design a lifestyle that was once only a dream.

This book will show you how. It will show you how others are doing it, why travelers are responding so positively, and how you can translate their satisfaction into your own opportunity. You may find it easier than you ever imagined to enter this marketplace and delight vacationers, creating your own prospects for traveling, meeting people, and designing the life that you've always wanted to have.

***

My first introduction to vacation rentals was as a guest, not as an owner. My wife, Dani, and I are passionate world travelers who have both lived abroad. We were eager to pass along some of that enthusiasm to our young son, and so we planned family excursions that we hoped would generate the spark. But there was always something missing. Somehow, those trips fell just short of our expectations. I don't recall who steered us toward a privately owned vacation rental instead of a hotel stay, but in 2005 we booked a private home in the historic Centro of San Miguel de Allende, Mexico, for 10 days. It was a revelation!

First of all, San Miguel is one of the most beautiful cities in Mexico — rife with distinct colors, scents, people, and a comfortable pace of life… Staying in a private home let us melt into the city and the neighborhood instead of always bumping into hotel staff. There was no noise from the hallway at three o'clock in the morning and no one constantly pestering us to "upgrade our vacation package." We just immersed ourselves into our surroundings. We found our own rhythm and a new way of seeing things. We decided then and there that we would never go back to a hotel unless there was no other option.

It felt unusual to be staying in someone else's home, and it became an adventure. Exploring the property was as much fun as exploring the city. Our hosts had furnished the place so thoughtfully, with beautiful artwork and photographs, sculptures, and walls full of books. No hotel had ever come close, and the modest rates made it affordable for a family with a young child.

Dani and I had enrolled in authentic Mexican culinary classes in San Miguel, in which you could train with masters for an hour or two. Thanks to our vacation rental, we could then hit the markets for fresh ingredients and go "home" to re-create what we had just learned, in "our" kitchen. ¡Qué delicioso! We were able to extend the moment and our exhilaration in the culture. That would not have been possible in a hotel — we were truly able to bring the city home with us. We found a local school that welcomed daytime drop-ins, so our son had the opportunity to play and interact with local Mexican kids for a few hours every afternoon as Dani and I explored more of the sights, sounds, and tastes of San Miguel. We wished it would never end.

Joel Rasmussen

As we watched our son make friends, learn some of the language, and develop opinions and observations about our temporary new home, we knew that we had discovered a way of traveling and experiencing the world that would be life changing for all of us. We wanted to share that excitement with others. Not long afterwards, we would get our chance to make that vision a reality.

Back in Austin, Texas, our primary business had been purchasing homes, renovating them, and reselling them at an appreciated value. We enjoyed the work and the satisfaction of "recycling" dwellings that would improve other people's quality of life. We worked out of a small cottage near our home, not realizing the true value of this office space — until a good friend urged us to consider turning it over for a profit. "Buyers would love it. It's so cute, and close to all the tourist attractions. Its charm is wasted as your office," our friend chided us. We looked at each other and knew he was right.

But we had become attached to the little bungalow, and couldn't quite let it go. We decided instead to try renting it for short stays. When this proved successful, we realized that we could keep the property for its income stream. We didn't have to sell it. And so we stepped into a new career… one that would eventually lead to a new way of life.

***

In a few short years, we planned and scraped and saved; we learned more about management, and when the time came, we were able to take advantage of opportunities to buy several more properties. These needed only a little love and ingenuity to turn them into the type of vacation homes that we would be proud to stay in as well as rent out. That first experience in San Miguel had given us a feel for what travelers want. People who would opt for a vacation rental over a hotel want the comforts of home, but also the extra touches that they can't get in their everyday spaces, which always become cluttered with the "stuff" and obligations of daily life.

Dani and I knew how to create that extra-special environment. We chose to cluster our properties near where we lived, offering what we love about the city to guests, and keeping our workload manageable. This strategy resonated with nearly everyone who came to stay with us. We heard great comments, from "I totally fell for Austin on this stay…" to "…One of the top five places we have stayed — from India to Cayman Island, New York, San Francisco…" and "The house is full of little touches that make it feel like staying at a friend's place…" and "How lucky were we to stay at this amazing property!"

The concept took off, and the dynamic of welcoming newcomers, yet giving them the privacy and atmosphere they needed in order to relax, was one that fit right in with our personalities and work styles. In short, we loved what we were doing. But we had never lost our desire to capture that feeling for ourselves, and the income would give us the freedom to travel more and more, as our son grew older.

What we discovered, and what we offer to guests at our rentals, is the chance to expand the meaning of a vacation. Simple time off or time out can be immeasurably enriched by the discovery that comes with the best form of travel — even short-distance travel, close to home. Let's face it: We are all creatures of habit, and travel takes us out of that safe orbit to meet people with different traditions, amazing talents, and new points of view. Yes, this can happen while staying at a hotel — but those boundaries inevitably restrict us.

Humans are social creatures. Still, we also need personal space to process our impressions in real time — not waiting until we check out of the hotel a week later and go home to tell our friends what happened, if we can remember. Staying in a private home lets us sit down at the end of the day and really savor the unique sights, sounds, and experiences that we encountered a few hours earlier, and to share tales of the days' adventures with our companions. There are no waits in the elevator and parking garage, no interruptions in the conversation. It doesn't matter whether we travel across the globe or down the block, in this setting, the smallest insight can become a lasting memory.

And so our new business became an outlet for our passion on this subject. We added properties, dressed them up, and brought in like-minded guests whose experience of Austin became an extension of our rental spaces. As my family did on that ground breaking San Miguel trip, our guests melted into the culture. The response has been overwhelmingly positive, and it represents just a small subset of the vacation rental industry, which is seeing phenomenal growth each year. This is how people want to spend their hard-earned time and money. This is how people want to travel.

Then, just as the future seemed bright and secure, a local dispute threw the business of short-term rentals in our area into chaos. A challenge mounted by a few misinformed and disgruntled residents became an effort to outright ban vacation rentals in the city. Wild imaginings by some nervous homeowners painted short-term rentals as fronts for drug operations, brothels, and even wilder unknown — and unfounded — illicit doings. Tempers flared, opponents organized, and before we knew it, our very existence hung by a thread.

***

I realized we had to tell our side of the story or quickly face financial ruin, so I formed an association and invited other vacation rental owners to join. Even though we were ostensibly competitors, we had a lot to gain by working together, and could possibly even lose our rental businesses if we didn't. We were honest taxpayers, providing valuable services and generating significant revenue for the local economy. We had the right to handle our properties as we saw fit, as allowed by the law. With our combined forces as the Austin Rental Alliance — and with backing from the owners and employees of Internet listing service HomeAway and the Austin Board of Realtors— we worked with the city to craft fair regulations that would let us continue to fill the demand for short-term rental accommodations.

I learned how to handle the challenges that rental property owners across the country are facing and how to craft effective regulations that make everybody happy. I went on to accumulate a very profitable and successful vacation rental operation in Austin, and that expertise has allowed me to help other people do the same. My association with HomeAway is not a paid endorsement, but a mutually beneficial partnership meant to preserve the legal right for owners—and vacationers—to provide and to choose the type of accommodations that they prefer.

That drama may soon be a thing of the past, as municipalities realize a surge in revenue from the taxes and local spending stream that vacation rentals produce. All that's left for those of us who have made a career of delighting travelers is to find the best way to do so, dealing with the day-to-day aspects of running a personally satisfying business. By reading this book you will discover how to profitably own, market, and manage vacation rental properties too.

But you don't have to follow in my footsteps. My story is just one in thousands. There is no single way to successfully manage a career or a second income in vacation rentals. It's a lifestyle that you can mold to your own strengths, hopes, and dreams. You can forge your own path. You can begin a journey that will take you many places.

I'll show you how to take the first step now. Come with me!

–Joel Rasmussen

CHAPTER 1

Is This for Me?

Why to rent…
What to rent…
Can I do it?

I f you're tossing around the idea of making a go at renting out a second property, you might think that money considerations are your top priority. Not so. The funds to buy and maintain a second home or multiple properties actually take a back seat to your personal goals in this decision. Your resources definitely figure into the equation—but your skill set, personality, and reasons for wanting to rent may be more important to whether you can be successful as a host.

Many small businesses fail because entrepreneurs and proprietors get emotionally caught up in the idea of an occupation, rather than its realities. For instance, new restaurants are notorious for failing to make it into the black within their first year. Why? Lack of expertise, poor market research, and unwillingness to put in long hours are just some of the reasons for financial collapse. But what is it that makes new restaurateurs think they can overcome these handicaps? Emotion. They get dreamy eyed with visions of opening up the perfect little place where they would like to dine, or of overseeing a busy venue to which customers flock to sample dishes like grandma used to make. While a passion for the business does play into success, running on unbridled emotion without concern for the laws of commerce is a sure way to doom a fledgling enterprise.

How can you find a happy medium between desire and reality to form your own vacation rental empire? It's simple: Look at both sides of the coin. Get excited about your prospects, yes. Then take a step back from that enthusiasm to consider whether your situation is conducive to running this type of business.

A Reasonable Rationale

Dreams surely keep us going, but realistic goals have the best chances of being realized. First off, ask yourself: Why do I want to host vacationers? If it's because you love meeting people, perfect. If it's to gain the flexibility to travel yourself, wonderful. If it's to increase your income or to switch sources of income, that's viable as well. One of these practical reasons is enough to engage you in long-term business.

Ambitions that include capitalizing on a down real estate market or making easy money for little effort, however, might not cut it. There are better ways to turn a profit in real estate than catering to short-term renters, and illusions of buying a second property and sitting back to wait for the rent checks to roll in are naive, at best. Managing a prosperous vacation rental takes steady work. It's satisfying work, but it is not a passive source of income.

That's not to say that your long-held desires should not play into this decision. If you have always wanted a vacation home for yourself but thought you couldn't afford one, renting out a property part of the year may gain you the funding to maintain a place that you can enjoy part time too. Such a prospect depends on many factors, including property location, your financial and management skills, and the economy — but it absolutely can be done.

These elements also figure into goals of bringing in enough money to travel or engaging with new people who will enrich your life with new social and cultural experiences. But your fundamental reasons for striking off on a vacation rental endeavor must be the driving force behind it all. If you enjoy traveling and meeting people from around the world, then I can't think of a better reason to own a rentable property. It's a fantastic way to get to know people from different backgrounds. Supplementing your income or even to changing careers are also very achievable goals when you succeed in this business.

Be honest with yourself from the get-go. Keep asking yourself that bottom-line question: Why do I want to do this? If you remain firm in your rationale, then you'll know it's probably a good one.

Assets and Resources

The next practical consideration is what you have to offer demanding travelers. You do need a dwelling place to rent out. Do you already own a second property or buildable land, or a granny flat at your primary residence? If not, do you regularly vacation elsewhere, leaving your own home available to potential renters during certain times of the year? Is there a big event in the city you live in that brings in a large volume of travelers? If so, perhaps you can pay for that trip to Paris that you've been wanting to take by renting out your personal residence during that time. Or maybe you just want to make some extra money to pay for upcoming repairs or taxes on your home. You might go camping for the weekend while guests rent your place. If you'd rather purchase a separate home, what is your credit standing?

Even if you are not a good loan prospect from the bank's perspective, your avenues to gaining a second property are not closed. I know people who have started out by leasing property and become successful. They may have signed a five-year lease on a less-desirable home, invested the expense and the time to improve it, and turned around to sublease it to travelers on a short-term basis. These opportunities are limited, but they do exist. Keep in mind that if this is your plan you must be absolutely clear about it with the landlord, and also make sure regulations in your area allow sublets.

If you own a spare property or make it your business to acquire fixer-uppers, you already have a foot in the door. Why sell for a one-time profit when you can rent for an ongoing income? A traditional rental property I know of was recently purchased was bringing in about $900 in monthly rent at the time of the sale. Now it averages around $5,000 a month as a short-term rental. So, even in a slow economy, the market is compelling. As long as people continue to travel or take close-to-home vacations, there will be a potential pool of renters.

Yes, an investment is definitely needed up front, both in acquiring real estate or a habitable dwelling and in bringing it up to a certain level of comfort. I attribute part of my success to a willingness to furnish a place beyond what travelers expect — to wow them. While you do need a margin of funds or credit to be able to do so, another of your resources is just as crucial: your time.

***

You may be well set financially, but you'll need to be able to make a firm time commitment in getting your property ready to rent and doing all the things necessary to get a business off the ground. You may be thinking, "Can't I hire someone to do the ground work?" Certainly, you can "buy" some help. But only you should perform the background work and make the hard decisions that precede welcoming your first renters. We'll talk more about real estate financing and paid versus self-management options in the next few chapters. In most cases, though — and contrary to popular opinion — you cannot buy time.

Continue with your honest interior dialogue. Does my job leave chunks of free time in the evenings or weekends? Do my family obligations or hobbies still allow me extra time? Is early retirement an option in order to free up time? If you answer "no" to all of these questions, you will have to go back to the drawing board. If you plan to share the burden of time and effort with a spouse or partner, explore those questions together. Expect a large time commitment to start with, and move toward a manageable workload from there.

How long will it take, at first? If you are renting out a portion of your own home, the busy work can be done on weekends and by putting in extra weekday hours. If your rental property is located a distance from your home, getting back and forth will add to the time requirement. A property that needs to have a fair amount of renovation done will increase your hourly outlay as well. In addition to estimating that time period and whether you will be free, you must decide if you are willing to give up your downtime — at least in the initial project stages. To me, the rewards on the other end are so worth it. Once you have the property listed, renters coming in, and revenue and feedback flowing, the enterprise is completely worth the time and effort, from my point of view.

Suppose you get over the first hump. Should you be nervous about signing away your free time in the future? Not really. You'll be able to make your own schedule before long. Vacation rentals offer you the flexibility to design your lifestyle, which I find to be the most enjoyable aspect of owning them. Some people get so into the work that it can become a full-time occupation. It doesn't have to be, of course. If you just want to supplement your income — maybe help pay for your taxes or your own vacations — then the job can be managed effectively in a few hours per week. If you opt to use a property management firm and you outsource all the renovation, then it takes almost no time at all once you get established. We'll talk more about the financial trade-offs of such an arrangement in later chapters. But for those who really want to make hosting a profession, full-time effort can reap full-time rewards. At this point, my wife, Dani, and I have multiple properties in Austin, and running them is our primary occupation. So with a little thought and effort, the time commitment can be what you choose.

***

Let's say that you have some money, and you have the time. Don't stop asking yourself the tough questions! Besides exploring your personal motivations for wanting to step into the vacation rental realm, you should next appraise your resources for actually transacting that business day to day, month to month, and over the long haul.

Personality and Skills

You may have decided, I want to do this. Now consider the make-or-break question: Can I do this?

It takes a certain type of person to be able to deal with new people, maintain a house, market a service, keep accurate books, and all of the many other details involved with hosting travelers. I'm not saying these are difficult things in and of themselves; together, they are tasks to which you may or may not be suited. To further assess your chances at success in the vacation rental business, let's look at your personality, your natural tendencies, and your skill set.

Are you a people person? Even if you are, can you handle difficult people? Can you handle them diplomatically yet firmly?

An overly shy proprietor might be a wonderful human being, but might not possess the ability to welcome strangers into her home or to bridge a language barrier. Conversely, someone who really enjoys meeting people, having conversations, and getting to know folks from other cultures, probably has the necessary curiosity and willingness to engage — traits that put guests at ease. Still, any owner who wants to be "nice" all the time might not be able to evict a problem tenant or even retain a security deposit for damaged property. These problems, though rare in my experience, do arise from time to time, and the longer you're in operation, the more likely it is that you will eventually have an unpleasant situation to handle. That's just part of any business. But, to keep your rental on track and making money — and to cultivate good relationships with neighbors and city law enforcement — you must be able to address people-related situations swiftly and effectively when they do occur.

So, consider the balance that you need to strike as a host, good neighbor, and businessperson in light of your own strengths and weaknesses. The remainder of this book will show you what kind of interpersonal skills you might need in the course of managing your rental property. Other major skills include powers of organization, the ability to keep books well, and a basic marketing sensibility. The latter two can be learned by most people. The first — organizational skills — are intuitive tendencies that may or may not be in your repertoire. If you are always hunting for receipts, missing appointments, or losing your car keys, managing a business like this may not be for you.

Again, you will get the big picture on which details need organizing as you read further. As far as taking care of a second property goes and the preparation for, and the aftermath of, guests — you can probably handle that stuff. Daily upkeep of a vacation property is no more complicated than running your primary household. You probably clean your home, pay your utility bills and mortgage, and balance your checkbook each month already. Adding income-tracking tasks to that accounting activity isn't much of a stretch. There are software programs that will help, and you can always take an introductory class in QuickBooks if you need to get up to speed. Alternatively, you can pay professionals to manage cleaning and maintenance of your rental property and to perform accounting services. As we will discuss, this type of outsourcing cuts into your profits, but that issue ties back into your primary goals: If you just seek a partial or supplementary income, that's fine. If you want to make a living and a lifestyle out of property ownership, then you will definitely want to cultivate these learnable financial skills.

While financial acumen, social smarts, and a knack for organization are important to running a rental enterprise, marketing savvy—or access to someone with it—is perhaps the most crucial aspect to becoming successful. After all, to keep money coming in, you first need to locate and lure prospective renters. Chances are that you won't do this by wearing a sandwich sign and marching up and down the block. Fortunately, marketing vacation rentals is easier today than it ever has been, and plenty of help is available. What is vital is your recognition of the importance of ongoing marketing and your readiness to work on it yourself or from the sidelines as long as you rent out your home. The vacation market changes, and if you sit still, your property will sit empty.

We'll talk more about marketing in Chapters Four and Five. Advertising your property isn't hard, once you get a feel for it. It just takes commitment. Now, your final point for consideration before starting a vacation rental business is whether your community regulations will allow it to be a profitable venture.

Rules and Regulations

I have already mentioned our challenges in the city of Austin over the legal right of property owners to share their dwellings with short-term guests. Obviously, it's legal to rent a home or apartment month to month. To my knowledge, no place in the United States prohibits that practice. But several jurisdictions, by city or county, do restrict the length and purpose of property rentals. For instance, Portland, Oregon, and New York City enacted ordinances that ban rentals shorter than 30 days. While some regulations might not be effective in keep owners from renting short term — Portland's and New York's stance only increased the number of listings for minimum-term rentals — they might keep you from making the size of profit that you seek.

Additionally, even though the practice of renting short term may be legal, other restrictions may apply. In Austin, for example, property owners need to register with the city and obtain a license. Unless they occupy the property as their primary residence, they're subject to a density limit on the total number of licenses issued in a given census tract — there is no limit on the number of owner-occupants who can get a license, but they are limited to renting no more than sixty days per year. In order to learn about industry regulations in your area, check with your local city government. There should be an information desk you can call or a web page you can access to get the specifics.

Need help? I've been directly involved in the launch of an online resource for vacation rental owners called STRAdvocacy.org. The site allows you to contact other owners and to read about their ongoing challenges, as well as solutions, for keeping their short-term rental rights. You can review best practices from other parts of the country and around the world online. STRAdvocacy.org was created with the help of rental listing sites HomeAway, FlipKey, and Airbnb—another key example of "competitors" joining forces for the benefit of everyone in the vacation rental industry.

To learn more I spoke with Matt Curtis, director of government relations at HomeAway. "Throughout the country and around the world there are regulations that could affect short-term rentals," he told me. "Owners need to be aware of the ordinances in their area and be prepared that if they don't currently have regulations they may soon, so it's important to know what's going on now as well as what could happen in your community. The easiest way to stay ahead of the curve is to get organized," he said. "Find out from owners, managers, and other stakeholders in your area what regulations might be in place now or if anyone was talking about putting new regulations in place. Regulations pop up very quickly, and the best way to know what is happening is to have a lot of ears to the ground. I strongly recommend being involved in a local owners' alliance, or if one doesn't exist, to take advantage of the opportunity to form one."

Regarding hard-and-fast legal obligations, as an operator of a short-term rental business, you will need to meet local and state tax codes as well as comply with the Fair Housing Act and Americans with Disabilities Act. These requirements are not as complicated as you might think. Here are the basic rules:

City/county/state hotel tax. In most jurisdictions overnight stays are subject to a per-night occupancy tax, which may vary by state, county, or city—or which may be payable to all three. The charge may be called a bed, room, tourist, accommodation, or hotel tax, or another name that means the same thing. The tax is levied against the renter, not the owner. However, your job as owner is to collect that tax from your customers and forward it to the tax authorities, usually quarterly or monthly. That means you collect it, hold it briefly without spending it, and send it on as required. Yes, there are professional service that will help you do this. More on that later.

Fair Housing Act

Although you are free to screen prospective renters and choose who may stay at your property, according to the amended version of the 1968 Civil Rights Act, you may not base your decision on the "race, color, national origin, religion, sex, familial status or handicap" of those in question. That means you can't bar people of certain races, nationalities, religions, and genders, and you can't turn away parents with kids or people with disabilities based solely on those criteria.

Who's to know? Anyone from the neighbors to your listing service, all the way up to the U.S. Department of Housing and Urban Development, which polices the industry for discriminatory practices. If you make a business of renting out your space, you won't want to risk losing the right to profit from it.

Americans with Disabilities Act

This legislation was enacted in 1990, in part to remove barriers to building access for people whose mobility is limited by a disability (ADA Title III). In general, homes built prior to July 1992 do not have to meet accessibility standards, while those built afterwards may have to. The guidelines were updated in March 2012, so depending upon the construction date of your home, you may have different obligations that might include removing stairways, widening doors, or other fixes. You can call the ADA Information Line at 800-514-0301 to find out where you stand as a property owner.

***

By staying up to date with these obligations, you will stay out of trouble with the courts, the Internal Revenue Service and state and local tax boards—and you'll demonstrate good business practices to thwart arguments against vacation rentals. There are other less stringent legal considerations, such as those associated with hiring service people and complying with neighborhood and homeowner's association regulations. These might include filing 1099 tax forms, maintaining your lawn regularly, and keeping guest noise within bounds. Those are duties that everyone faces, and you can too.

If you've read this far, you probably have a basic sense of

whether the vacation rental business is for you. Continue to assess how appropriate your skills, strengths, and resources are for the job as you read on. But this may be the point to determine whether or not you can seriously consider this opportunity. Try it now: Decide to decide!

***

You Might Ask...

Q. Can I use my existing home as a vacation rental?

A. Absolutely. That's how many owners get started. You'll need an alternative residence — maybe you can stay with friends or family a few weeks or months during the busy season. We have a neighbor who stays with friends when he gets a booking, or if it's far enough in advance, he'll schedule his own business travel in order to make his home available. How can you do it? Get creative and think of all the fun and interesting options that could turn your home into a part-time moneymaker.

Q. Do I have to give up my day job?

A. You don't. But when you are starting out, you will probably want to use some vacation time or a break in seasonal work to put in the hours it will take to start a business.

Q. Do I need to live in the same area as my rental house?

A. No. But you will need to budget more time and expense for travel back and forth to check on and maintain the property if you don't live nearby. We have good friends who live overseas and rely on local services for cleaning, occasional handyman work, and dealing with emergencies. They've also hired a local who works a few hours per week as their concierge to liaison with guests. If you live out of the area, though, consider that you might need to make emergency trips to your property every now and then.

CHAPTER 2

Is There a Market?

Where to rent…
Who will rent…
Can I profit here?

When considering a new business venture, before shelling out investment funds and opening the doors, performing market research is a must. You might have a dynamite place and special services to offer, but if a market doesn't exist, you can still go belly-up. Even if a pool of renters is a sure thing, bringing them in as your paying customers is not. The local market may be flooded with properties. Other owners may offer more for less. Your property might not meet the standards of discerning travelers. Or, you might not encounter any obstacles and simply hit the ground running, thanks to a prior look into the local rental climate. Luck favors the prepared, so let's have a look.

Your initial market research should cover much more than simply an estimate of the number of potential renters. Meeting criteria of a desirable destination, enough interested parties, and an attractive property still will not ensure rental inquiries and bookings. How much active marketing will you have to perform to catch the attention of your target renters? The answer is: as much as it takes. Putting your effort into the right areas initially will make the task easier down the road. Are you good at creating effective advertisements, or can you hire competent people to help you do so? In today's competitive vacation rental marketplace, the maxim "If you build it they will come" does not necessarily apply. We'll see what some of the experts in the industry have to say about the importance of investing in a good marketing plan in later chapters.

For now, though, early market research will tell you whether it's smart to get into the rental business in your area. You may be eager to choose and furnish a property, but first take the time to figure out whether you can hope to break even, let alone make money at the hosting game. Again, step back from your enthusiasm and let your rational mind take over. Ask: What location would be best for me? Who can I expect to attract? Will there be enough turnover to meet my financial goals? We'll explore these issues in greater depth throughout the book, but now is the time to make a valiant effort at reviewing the market in relation to your available time and budget.

The Best Location

The ideal spot for a vacation rental differs from owner to owner. For me, it's within a five-minute walk or a two-minute drive from my own home. For you, it might be a thousand miles away at a place you love, using a second property you are trying to hang on to. Some experienced hosts who have good management help can maintain vacation rentals around the globe, in areas to which they like to travel.

My family has stayed in many vacation rentals with different operating styles (all of them successful). Some examples are:

San Miguel, Mexico - The owners lived in Florida and had a local concierge/manager that greeted us. We had his contact info and knew he was close by in case we needed any help.

Nosara, Costa Rica - The owners lived in Colorado and had a management company take care of everything from the booking to greeting us and maintaining the property.

Coeur d'Alene, Idaho - The owner lived in the next state and was readily available via phone or email. We had the contact info for her housekeeper/assistant in case we needed immediate help.

Vancouver, Canada - The owner lived next door to his properties (several in one building), and we would often see him gardening and conversing with guests. He was very friendly, yet gave everyone their personal space.

In practical terms, it's clearly easiest to run your business in the same local area as your residence. You save on gas, travel time, and grief when you avoid long-distance commutes and management efforts. If you have a beloved property in the next state or on the opposite coast, however, the remote location still might serve you well even with the extra outlay — if it's in an area that other people want to visit and if you have a reliable concierge, assistant, or manager.

How can you find out whether tourists or other types of guests favor the location you are considering? First, use what you know about the place. Are there popular tourist attractions or seasonal draws? In Austin, for instance, the world-famous music scene is a year-round people pleaser, with huge spikes in tourist action during October's Austin City Limits music festival and March's SXSW music, film, and technology summit. That doesn't even count summertime and holiday tourists or people who travel for other reasons. When you add in the universities, colleges, and the fact that it's the state capitol, it becomes evident that this area is a popular destination for travelers.

Is yours? Here are few vacation destinations that can draw large numbers of tourists:

- snow sports areas
- waterfront anything
- sports arenas
- world-class casinos
- cultural centers
- state and national parks
- natural wonders
- amusement parks
- university campuses
- state capitals
- culturally significant cities

Do you live near any of these? Own property in these areas? Wish to acquire property there? If not, that's okay too. Vacationers don't always fit into neat categories, and your customers might have other reasons to get up and go. Buying a second property near your own home is a great way to get started if the market will support it.

With your top locales in mind, start researching how much short-term rental activity is going on there by browsing the vacation-rental listing sites online. The major ones at this time include HomeAway.com, VRBO.com (Vacation Rentals By Owner, a site owned by HomeAway but different enough in the traffic it receives that I recommend it), FlipKey.com, and Airbnb.com.

Hint: You don't want to be the first owner to rent in your area, especially if you're just getting started. That's an uphill climb that might never pay off. Why can't I be the first?, you might ask. If no one is currently renting near the location you choose, there is probably a good reason for it. It may be too far off the beaten path, lacking in services, or truly unattractive to the average traveler. The opposite condition — a plethora of short-term rentals nearby — is not necessarily a deal breaker. Whether that could be a lucrative location or not depends on the size of the customer base, but in general, a well-stocked market is a good sign.

Say you check out the listings and find a half dozen or dozens of homes for rent short term in your preferred location. Then consider how many seasons of the year you might expect occupancy. If it's primarily a ski area, you might see most renters during six months or less out of the year. If it's a beach front, you might be looking at similar numbers. Obviously, the winter and spring breaks and the summer months when school is out are the heaviest travel times. Passable roads, storm seasons, and local event schedules may also figure into when people can or will want to stay at your place.

Try this: Get a piece of paper and make two columns, one for attractions to renters, and one for impediments. Write down all the reasons that tourists might want to come to your area, and when. Then jot down all the reasons they might not want to be there at certain times. For instance, if you're thinking of a rental in southern Louisiana, February's Mardi Gras would be one attraction, while possible hurricanes in summertime might be an impediment. What might affect travelers' stays? Include unexpected conditions, from an early snow season to intermittent construction next door.

How do your two columns compare? Do the attractions outweigh or offset the obstacles to getting renters into your chosen location? If you're not sure, return to the online listings and see what other local owners are advertising. Most owners describe what their area holds for travelers — bird watching, hiking, access to famous landmarks, or what have you. Their ads let readers know whether their area is accessible year-round, or if roads might sometimes be closed by snow. If obstacles threaten your ability to rent in a certain place for much of the year, you probably won't see many homes advertised there.

On the other hand, the location that you choose may be a slam-dunk. An area near a popular lake, Disneyland, or a quaint seaside town might show dozens or even hundreds of vacation homes available. And don't discount urban properties. Those in San Francisco, Las Vegas, and other cities that are hot with tourists draw just as many vacationers as outlying areas. Scroll through the listings to the booking calendars to see what occupancy rates look like. (Note that these may be sparse in the early months of the year, before people get around to planning and booking their vacations.)

If it looks like others are doing well in the rental market in your chosen spot, and if you can get your hands on property there, then move on to the next part of the equation: Who is it that reserves short-term rentals there? Your chances for success and profits are directly related to whether there is enough interest by enough people who might want to rent from you.

Your Target Market

Your target market — all of your potential customers — is made up of every possible type of traveler who might make your location a destination. This pool may ebb and flow with the seasons or remain strong due to business opportunities or year-round tourist attractions. Some of the guests that you might see include:

- families that generally vacation on holiday weekends and in summertime
- teachers and college students celebrating short or long breaks
- individual business travelers in town for meetings or conferences
- other convention attendees
- corporate groups on retreats
- sports enthusiasts
- relatives visiting students, family members, or friends who live nearby
- singles or couples who prefer to travel in the off-season
- community residents displaced from their homes by fire, remodeling, or lapses between home sales and purchases
- artists on working vacations
- people attending sports matches, concerts, festivals, and other events

Review this list with your chosen location in mind. Which types of people are apt to want to stay in such a place? (This will help you answer many questions when you get around to advertising.) Does it sound like a lot of people? Now whittle away at that list — in consideration of how many of those folks will be viable renters.

Let's talk briefly about screening. Out of the sector of the general population who: a) want to come to your area; b) will select a vacation rental over a hotel or friend's couch; c) see your listing and like it; and d) actually make contact and firmly book a stay — the list of prospects will shrink even further. Who is your property right for? Who is right for your property?

When you list your rental and begin to get inquiries, you'll want to speak with potential renters by phone. This will weed out many who would rent a house for illicit purposes or run a scam for a refund without even renting at all. Most importantly, it will turn away those whom you don't want on your property, and whom you may legally ban. You might want to discourage renters such as:

- indoor smokers
- groups that are too large
- college kids on spring break
- people with destructive pets
- renters who might not be comfortable at your place
- someone who has already acted rude on the phone

I have a basic policy that I tailor my screening conversation around. I don't rent to anyone age 25 or younger, and I don't accept more than five people on a single property. That doesn't mean that I turn away larger groups; sometimes I can accommodate them at my side-by-side properties. And folks under 25 can stay, as long as the primary renters are of age and I feel that they are responsible. It's my call. We'll get into the nitty-gritty and legal issues of guest screening in Chapter Eight. The point is that, out of the general population, the number of potential renters that meet your requirements and you theirs will probably render your target market smaller than first estimated.

In order to close in on that core group, you'll have to think about your boundaries regarding to whom you will rent. Downsizing your target market is not always a losing proposition. Screening out folks who are not likely to enjoy your property can save you refunds, damages, and grief in the long run. A family of five won't be right for a one-bedroom cottage. An elderly or disabled person will not want to climb the ladder to your property's loft bedroom.

Now, get a piece of paper and write down notes about your final estimated target market. When you get a handle on the type of traffic you might see in a given year, you can consider how you will stack up against the competition. This will determine how busy you will be and whether you can achieve as many bookings as you need to turn a profit.

Your Competition

I have already mentioned that you don't want to be the first in your neighborhood to try to entice vacation renters. Of course, that means that you will have to compete with others who are trying to do the same thing. Isn't it possible that there will be enough renters to go around? If you live in a tourist-driven area, that may be so. But you should assume the opposite.

Although you will cultivate friendly professional relationships with other local owners and you may enjoy separate traveler niches—in the end, you will all be competing for the same general market share. Studying the competition will help you determine:

- Whether you can equal what other owners have to offer
- Whether you can exceed that benchmark
- Whether you can achieve your minimum occupancy quota to stay afloat

There are two major ways to get the information you need—browsing the vacation rental listings in your area, and getting to know rental property owners in person. Before you buy a property or make a marketing plan, do your homework online. Read through the area short-term rental listings with your businessperson hat on to assess the competition. Rental ads will help you find out:

- What comparably sized units are renting for
- What their occupancy rates are
- Which amenities they offer
- Whether their advertisements are effective (check booking calendars)
- How many positive reviews they have

Some websites, such as HomeAway.com, have biography sections about the owners themselves. Read these to see who is behind the more or less successful properties.

Remember those hard questions? Continue to be ruthless in asking yourself bluntly: Can I do better than they can? With the number of vacation rentals growing each year, doing as well as the next guy might not be enough to meet your quotas. As you form your revenue goals, acknowledge that you may have to overcome the competition to stay in business and stay profitable. For instance, a good night's sleep is extremely important to guests. If the majority of owners are advertising European bed linens, can you afford to do so too? Can you afford to upgrade to king-sized beds or memory-foam mattresses? Is regular lawn and garden care, frequent home maintenance, and top-notch cleaning service within your budget? If not, you may see bookings go to your neighbors instead of you. On the other hand — if the supply of budget rentals in your area is limited — you may discover a niche market for yourself.

Once you delve into hosting guests, you might want to gain the protection and support — and an inside look at the competition — that membership in a property owners' organization can bring. When our Austin rental market was threatened with a regulatory ban, I founded an official owners' alliance to counter the opposition. If you can't find one to join, you can do the same. You'll also find property owners answering questions in online forums and offering advice on hosted group pages at the major listing service websites. These people will be your allies — and your competitors. It's not a mutually exclusive relationship. You will learn a great deal by interacting, and so will they, and the end result will be an improvement in what you give guests and how well you transact business in your community.

So, let's say that you have an idea of where you want to rent, who might want to stay there, who you might want to host, and how many renters your area is supporting, divided among the ownership. Now that you are on your way to understanding how many bookings you might reasonably expect in your local marketplace, it's time to decide whether this venture will pay off to your satisfaction. Let's get down to the math of market research.

Your Bottom Line

If you're still running on emotional adrenaline, this is your last chance to get real before you decide whether you can make money at this venture. Even with the right property and a robust clientele, running a rental business is not a sure thing: The money you will bring in on a monthly basis may or may not offset your costs of doing business, especially as you are getting started. We haven't yet begun to factor in your expenses, from down payments and mortgages to electricity and toilet paper. Don't worry about those expenditures just yet. The bottom line you're looking for at this point is the number of weeks booked that are necessary to break even. You can continue to forge your income goals as you learn more, but you will have an early answer to whether or not you can avoid losing money at renting. "Yes" will mean read on. "No" will mean… keep reading, but don't quit your day job.

Remember those prices on local rentals that you looked up in the online listings? You can return to those pages to complete your preliminary market research. They will help you arrive at a per-night amount to charge. You may think your place is worth a million bucks, but that might not be what the market will bear. People are always looking for a better deal. In order to compete, you'll have to set an amount somewhere within the confines of the local price range.

Again, check the roster of rentals within a radius of your property that appear to be serving the same target market. If your property is near a vibrant downtown, a ski facility, or another attraction that draws tourists, consider the farthest distance from those points that folks might want to be based. For instance, Dad probably wouldn't want to drive longer than 30 minutes back to a home or hotel after a day with the kids at Disneyland—the shorter the transit time, the better, and the more you can charge to stay per night. Make sense? Inside the map boundaries that you choose, look for comparable properties by number of bedrooms and bathrooms, special features, and amenities. Get a feel for the range of nightly and weekly base rates and fees, taking note of the season. You will want your prices to be somewhere in that spread.

In the interest of full disclosure, most owners' ads list their entire pricing grid for the year. Take your time to learn about seasonal cash flow by comparing the prices in your area. If you have a two-bedroom condo, and if similar floor plans go for $100 a night in the off-season to double that in peak weeks, you will be able to calculate your potential gross income, or at least set high and low marks.

If you already own property, you know what mortgage, property tax, insurance, and basic maintenance costs run. This amount will be your "bottom" bottom line—the amount of money you would like to take in to be able to keep your property and make it pay for itself. Adding in your business expenses will give you the amount of money it will take to make the business of delighting travelers pay for itself while paying for the property. Above and beyond that… start thinking profit.

Go ahead and plug the numbers that you have into the range of potential rental income that you drafted. If there is some comfortable room in there, you just might have a winning prospect. You can also visit HomeAway.com and search among the Homeowners information section for a tool that will help you calculate a roughly estimated rental income.

***

In the following chapter, we'll talk about areas of the business in which you must invest in order to gain bookings and revenue—in other words, your foreseeable major expenses. This will show you how to put your money in the right places at the right time. Start-up and ongoing expenses may include:

- property purchases and renovations
- interior furnishings
- marketing and advertising
- professional services
- housekeeping and maintenance services
- administrative support
- daily supplies

As you can see, the list of business expenses is not short. But being proactive and investing enough to avoid lost income or big bills associated with repairs, liability issues, employment disputes, and dissatisfied guests can end up saving you money. Are you the type of person who is willing to service the washing machine rather than wait for it to break down? If not, do you think you can change? All of these personal and financial considerations play into whether you can succeed with vacation rentals.

Still enthusiastic? Keep going. By the time you finish reading this book, you will be able to realistically estimate your "top" bottom line — how many bookings and how much revenue you need to take in to run the business, turn a profit, and reach your personal financial goals. Don't stop asking yourself the hard questions until then.

***

You Might Ask...

Q. Should I buy a new or used property?

A. It's a matter of preference. Dani and I enjoy taking structures with "good bones" and fixing them up to see what can be done with them. In some ways, there's more flexibility in working with older homes than in starting from scratch. On the other hand, some people in our rental alliance buy new properties specifically to attract a certain type of guest.

Q. Should I join an owner's organization?

A. Once you get started, definitely. You will make friends and gain much-needed support from your "competitors." You might even attend a meeting or two while you are deciding whether to enter the business. On a day-to-day basis, I learn more about best practices, mistakes to avoid, and possible problems from my fellow rental alliance members than from any other source. We have a tight-knit group that is eager to share tips with each other — and more importantly watch each other's backs. We'll talk about Craigslist and the world of scams in Chapter 4.

Q. Will I have a say in who rents my house?

A. If you stick with the major listing sites that allow you to control the transaction, such as HomeAway, VRBO, and FlipKey, you retain the right to screen potential guests. Some rental listing sites, like Airbnb, make contact between renters and owners more difficult prior to a stay. If you handle all your bookings through your own personal website or by emailing or faxing contracts, you have the final word.

CHAPTER 3

Where Should I Start?

What to include…
What to ignore…
What are my priorities?

Now that I have shown you how to assess your readiness, willingness, and ability to take on a vacation rental business, the decision to move forward is yours. For the remainder of this book, I'll assume that your decision is YES. Another given will be the choice to take on management of the day-to-day business yourself. As you will see, this gives you the greatest chance of maximizing your profit. If you don't go that route, you will still need to know what to ask of the professionals that you hire, so read on.

Because owners also need vacations, let's assume that you will, from time to time, outsource this management work so you can take a break. That's fine. An individual contractor or service can stand in for you — fielding phone calls, taking bookings, managing cleaners — when you travel or are busy entertaining personal house guests, or when other projects interfere with your work schedule. Remember, one of your goals is to design your own lifestyle around this enterprise. But to keep your finger on the pulse of your business, in general, you will want to do two things: run as much of it as possible yourself and stay in your rental property every now and then.

After performing initial market research and deciding to take the plunge, get a good real estate agent and financial planner, if necessary, to secure your first rentable property. Or work with a trusted contractor to assess a current property for any renovation it might need to bring it up to par. Then, hang onto your hat: You're about to start spending money. This chapter will help you determine what to invest in, what to avoid, and — most importantly — what to do first.

Think Like a Traveler

What's that? You've never stayed in a vacation rental home yourself? Then, before you get down to business, it's time to take a vacation. Even if you can't actually get away just now, you can plan a vacation up to the departure point. The point of the exercise is to get you thinking like a traveler.

Go back to your list of all of the potential types of guests you think you might see. Then plan a trip — or plan several trips — putting yourself in their shoes. You will find as you go through the steps yourself that all vacation and business-trip planners want:

- An easy way to browse and book accommodations
- A fair and secure payment procedure
- A clear knowledge of the property layout
- A sense that their money will be well spent

Travelers who opt for vacation homes rather than hotels also expect a certain level of comfort, depending on the type of lodging and the guests' purpose for being in the area. (For example, rustic furnishings might be great for a fishing trip but wrong for a honeymoon suite.) Business and pleasure travelers want:

- Surroundings as good as — or better than — what hotels provide
- Homey extras like washer/dryers and fully equipped kitchens
- Comfortable beds with clean linens
- Reliable, high-speed internet access
- Cable TV with lots of channels

Some people are planning landmark celebrations for occasions like weddings, honeymoons, or family gatherings. This may be the trip of a lifetime for them. Special-event travelers want unique luxuries, such as:

- patios or decks for entertaining
- upscale decor
- great views
- privacy

Getting started in the vacation rental business will entail addressing all of these criteria to gain the widest audience of potential guests. Additionally, some people will have special needs that not every type of accommodation satisfies. If you can offer the extras they need, you can gain extra bookings. Consider making your property accessible for disabled travelers, secure for pets, or especially kid friendly. I'll address these topics more fully in the next volume in this series. At first, though, place your investments where they will satisfy the majority of renters. These may be investments in marketing, furnishings, or the property itself.

Don't worry about what you can't afford or can't find space for yet. Prioritize. Let's take travelers' most-pressing needs, wants, and wishes one a time.

Meet Their Needs

In order to meet the above objectives, focus on the big draws before buying knickknacks for the mantelpiece. Satisfy trip planners and the average traveler first:

1. Make it easy to find your ad and book a stay. When you're starting out, advertise where you will get the most for your dollars. This means subscribing to the most-popular listing sites, such as HomeAway, FlipKey, and VRBO. We will talk more about advertising in Chapters Four and Five, but subscribing to more than one listing service is the way to go — it increases your chances of people finding you, and vacation planners like the easy means of comparing properties and then booking them through these sites. So, make them happy from step one.

   As you branch out in marketing to taking your own bookings through a personal website (another topic for Volume Two in this series), you can use an online service such as VacationRentalDesk.com to help you keep your booking calendar up to date, as the major listing sites may do for you. That key service helps you achieve maximum occupancy. Browsers want to know if a property is available for the dates they are considering — immediately. Wouldn't you?

You will also need to work out a method for accepting bookings. The usual progression is: rental inquiry; screening phone call or email; and initiation of payment in exchange for your promise to rent space. Keep this system as simple as can be, to create the fewest possible steps between an inquiry and a reservation.

2. Use a secure payment system. Decide how you want to receive your payments, and lay it all out in writing in multiple places. Renters might read your payment policy on your listing site ad, a personal website, in an email, or in any paperwork that you might send them. You can have brochures made up that detail everything about your vacation rental and include payment terms there as well.

A common requirement by many owners is: 50 percent of the total (including base rate, cleaning fee, taxes, and security deposit) upon booking, with the balance payment due 30 days prior to arrival. A signed rental agreement will take care of any refund issues for cancellations. Guests also want peace of mind regarding the form of payment. Credit cards and PayPal online transfers are the most secure ways to give and receive payment. (Checks can bounce, and they keep you running to the bank as they come in.) At this writing, FlipKey and HomeAway offer online payment services that include check handling, which does save on merchant credit-card fees. Take some time to fully explore the options covered by your listing subscriptions; the rental websites use customer demand to create new services all the time.

3. Use photos and written content in ads to fully describe your property. Again, think like a traveler: Wouldn't you want to know whether your hotel or rental has things like separate bedrooms, a tub versus a shower, street or garage parking, stairs, a place to sit outdoors, and a million more details? I'll offer you expert advice on putting together the most effective advertisements in the following chapters, but you should start considering how you will present your property to potential renters right away.

   With all the choices available today, vacation planners want to know everything, so they can compare properties and pick the best one for their needs and tastes. Giving them the big picture on your rental home boosts you ahead of poorly described properties in the minds of those browsing the listing sites. A complete description also helps to discourage folks who might not be comfortable or satisfied with what you have to offer — the type of travelers who might cause trouble or write bad reviews. As you will see in our marketing discussion, your success may hinge on the quality of reviews that you get. Part of satisfying guests is to ensure that they are well suited to your property, and this encourages great reviews.

4. Compose ads that present your house as outstanding. Your ad is not a laundry list — it's a seductive story. Travelers these days have more options than ever in where to stay. And the competition in the short-term rental market in your area may be fierce. As you furnish and ready your home for guests, consider how you will capitalize on the strengths of the property in an ad. When you get around to writing your listing text, you'll want to fill in all the details, including physical features and location. But those considerations should come second to telling a really good story that draws readers in and takes them on a mini-vacation through your property before they ever leave their browsers.

Nobody wants to stay someplace that's "just good enough" on their vacation. Even folks who can only afford budget lodging still want the best place they can get, and they want to feel like they're getting a great deal for their money. Give it to them in writing. No other home is situated where yours is or is furnished in the same way. Play up what is special and unique about your property in your listing. If you wonder what that is, go stay there for a few days. Have friends walk through, and listen to their comments and first impressions. In writing your listing, get passionate about what you love in the area as you describe things to do nearby. Share your excitement about being a host on a bio page. Welcome readers and give them the feeling that this will be the best destination they have ever visited.

5. Provide clean, comfortable surroundings and friendly, professional service. Whether your decor is rustic, eclectic, chic, or funky, travelers will expect a certain level of atmosphere and comfort — and they will feel most comfortable dealing with owners who take their businesses seriously. Like it or not, they have certain expectations that have been set by the hotel industry. Think about it: Would you want to spend your money on a room or a home that is dusty, dirty, or foul-smelling? Overly austere or impossibly cluttered? Has a host ever made you feel uneasy by getting too intimate, seeming too disorganized, or making off-color jokes?

    If you read the online hotel reviews, most guest complaints revolve around surroundings that were not clean or comfy, and service that didn't measure up. Read the guest reviews on major hotel websites, Hotels.com, and TripAdvisor.com (it's fun!). As you create your daily business plan, keep hotel standards in mind. Put your money into reliable housekeeping services, quality furniture, and periodic maintenance. Cultivate a businesslike attitude that leaves room for personal attention but doesn't come on too strong. No one wants to feel that they are fueling your "hobby."

You can practice making a good first impression by role-playing phone calls, so that your answers to guest inquiries and your screening process are effective but not off-putting, gracious yet professional.

6. Keep on site laundry and kitchen appliances in working order. Putting your old washing machine or used kitchen appliances and utensils in your rental won't thrill your guests. In order to compete with homes that have top-of-the-line or at least well-kept laundries and kitchens, you will need to install new, quality models and make sure they work well week after week. Here is where a substantial initial investment—and extended warranties—will pay off.

    For major appliances, buy the best quality you can afford. This reaps returns threefold: fewer break-downs and repair bills; less-frequent replacements; and high guest wow factor. Imagine yourself going to wash your vacation clothes or make breakfast in your rental. How different would your reactions be to a new, clean washing machine and a used model with only half the cycles working? How about the prospect of cooking on a gas restaurant-style stove versus a hot plate? For similar aesthetic reasons, plan to replace kitchen utensils when they start to lose their luster. Would you rather make eggs in a like-new nonstick pan or one with the Teflon coating wearing off and a handle that jiggles?

7. Replace or upgrade beds, mattresses, and linens before they appear worn. The National Consumer Research Institute noted in 2012 that 76 percent of Americans want to raise the quality and quantity of their sleep. No wonder luxury mattresses are right up there on travelers' lists. Cleanliness counts, too, and sometimes "worn" is associated with "dirty."

    When it comes to beds, think about hotel reviews again. Some of the most… passionate comments have to do with the quality of the beds. If they are sumptuous, people gush. If they are not comfortable, many people vow never to stay at that hotel again. The same goes for linens. Have you ever stayed at a good hotel that did not make up its beds with like-new sheets and duvets?

Linens will be an ongoing expense, but type and quality of material are critical. Buy the highest thread-count sheets and pillowcases you can afford on a regular basis. If they are designer or European made, you can advertise that in your listing. When buying bed linens, towels, and wash cloths, look for high-grade cotton or poly/cotton blends that resist wrinkles and are bleach friendly — not that you want to use bleach in the wash cycle. Many hair and facial care products now have chlorine- or peroxide-based bleaching agents in them. If your guests use these products, your sheets or towels can be instantly ruined. Choose color-fast linens that don't react to bleach. Nothing is worse than seeing bleach stains on linens just after they were purchased.

8. Offer the best internet service and cable-TV packages that you can. People's whims may change tomorrow, but right now, travelers want to be connected. Especially if they are staying in a private residence, they will want internet and cable service as good as or better than theirs at home. Folks looking to get away from it all will make exceptions, of course, in exchange for the solitude, but even then, most people at remote properties would take an internet connection if they could get one — preferably high-speed, and preferably wireless.

    This is a realm in which privately managed vacation rentals can steal business from hotels. Again, if you read the hotel reviews, major complaints involve slow, spotty, or no internet service, and having to pay a surcharge for WiFi or dial-up connections. Grab those customers with a clear conscience: Offer unlimited wireless internet access, if possible, and don't charge extra for it. Just figure it into your overall budget. Do the same with cable TV channels, which can keep vacationers happy during inclement weather.

Exceed Their Expectations

In order to rise above the competition, instead of filling your home with more "stuff," add a few big wow factors. Excite discerning and special-event travelers next:

9. Create special indoor or outdoor entertainment areas. Think photo ops and quality lounge time in considering which areas of your property to turn into focal points. Who wouldn't want to dine on a beautifully landscaped patio, have a drink near the pool, or barbecue on a really gorgeous deck? You can attract your share of the special-occasion crowd by creating feel-good areas where your guests can relax or gather. These spots can also be set up indoors — a killer home theater, a sitting nook near French doors, or a lavish formal dining room.

    Outdoor gardens, water features, swimming pools, saunas, fire pits, and other dazzling spots can give guests what they don't have at home, and what they can't get at many hotels. Return to the online short-term rental and hotel listings to see what other properties are featuring. What makes you swoon? What do you envision at your property that could generate this sensation?

10. Personalize your space with quality furnishings. Custom decor and furnishings arranged as only you can provide also give guests what they cannot get at home or in most hotels. Design your home interior and exterior with a theme in mind, not as a resting place for you unwanted items. Part of the allure of my family's first stay in that vacation rental in San Miguel was the artfully decorated space. From the paint colors to the floor coverings, furniture,

fixtures, and artwork, the effect transported us from everyday life to another plane.

Even if you are going for a down-to-earth look, achieve it using materials that are interesting, well made, and well chosen. They don't necessarily have to be expensive. Here's a chance to consider how the average hotel decorates — and do the opposite. Your extra effort and expense in this area will add to the overall effect and impression that your property makes on guests, and could be the tipping point that results in enthusiastic referrals and many return bookings.

11. Highlight great views. Depending on your location, your property will either lend itself to special views or not. I don't have to tell you that a lovely beach, mountain, or skyline view is an ideal selling point. The best vacation properties, however, know how to make the most of them. Keep picture windows and window dressings clean. Set up a café table and chairs facing a picturesque pond or serene garden display.

What about non-view property? Well, there must be something pleasant to look at somewhere on the place. If not, create it. A rock waterfall. Hanging flower baskets. A whimsical mural. You get the picture. If you want more high-end customers, give them the perfect place for a honeymoon or anniversary getaway. A memorable setting generates word-of-mouth buzz… and repeat bookings.

12. Balance privacy with security. No matter what style your guests are seeking, there is one feature that makes people choose vacation rental properties over hotels time and again — added privacy. This doesn't have to mean seclusion, although some folks do want that sense of retreating from the mainstream. Fixes as simple as a fence, a hedge, or a decorative screen may do the trick in creating privacy boundaries that still let your guests blend into the neighborhood.

Privacy also means being free from intrusion by you and your service staff. Guests should know about your key policy, and feel confident that no one will make surprise visits, as a general rule. They will want to hear from you and perhaps interact with you — but they will want you to do your job. They'll expect you to go on your way without prodding. It may take some practice to achieve this balance between being a welcoming host and hovering, so take note of how others in the hospitality industry do this when you dine out or travel.

Stay Within Your Budget

The list above will help you understand where to start investing in your property and operations, and how to determine what needs ongoing attention from your wallet. When you figure out your income and expense limits, the resulting budget will help you prioritize what to buy and when to buy it. Use the photos and amenities listed on the short-term rental and hotel listing sites to get ideas and build wish lists.

Exercise restraint. Money may be tight when you're first starting out, so don't think that you have to furnish your property to the nines from day one. In fact, top-of-the-line everything may not be wise in the long run. Some things — like linens and kitchen utensils that get a lot of use — will have to be replaced on a regular basis, and it may not be feasible to buy luxury and gourmet quality every time. As long as you start with items of reasonably good quality and keep them clean and in working order, middle-range sheets, pots and pans, small electronics, and other home items will be fine for most guests. It is when things start to malfunction or show wear or stains that people notice.

You can always upgrade as you go along. And you will discover which brands or styles of furniture, appliances, and other necessities last and look good the longest. As you prioritize your wish list, focus on the high-demand items first. In my experience, the top five amenities that people want are:

- really comfortable beds
- wireless internet service
- cable television
- well-stocked kitchens
- good laundry facilities

So, if you want to please most of the people most of the time, resolve to pay the WiFi and cable bill monthly, service your appliances regularly, and buy new mattresses when needed. Among the things you do not absolutely need to have are land-line telephones (most people bring their own phones, but a land line may be necessary if the area has poor cell reception), DVD players (you've got cable, and most guests bring a laptop or iPad), and hot tubs (depending on your location).

As you decide how much to spend on prepping your property and running your business, do not discount the equal importance of investing your effort on a daily basis. Of all the things that go into making your vacation home comfortable and inviting, your positive and welcoming attitude may make the biggest impression on guests— and costs you nothing. It is your unique hosting ability that really makes your rental stand out from others. If you get overwhelmed by spending or by the limitations of your budget, remember that it's how well you treat your guests that should ultimately be your number-one priority.

***

You Might Ask...

Q. Are guest cancellations covered under payment terms?

A. Yes. Include in your stated terms how much (if any) of prepayments will be refunded in the event of cancellation — and why. Travelers are used to being able to opt out of a hotel reservation within 24 hours of check-in. In our business, we let people know that canceling a vacation rental reservation may mean a total loss of revenue for us if we can't fill that slot, unlike hotels that have multiple guest accommodations to offset a loss. We promise to refund as much of their prepayment as possible if we're able to re-book. If not, we offer partial refunds for cancellations made 30 days prior to the reserved date.

A solution to emergencies that threaten to kill a vacation investment is low-cost travel insurance that covers trip cancellation. If guests can't make their reserved dates or have to leave my property suddenly, they might not be able to recoup their money from me, but travel insurance can reimburse them. I spoke more about this with George Meshkov, president of insurance provider Customized Service Administrators. "Vacation rentals present an interesting departure from some established practices in the travel industry, particularly with cancellation policies," he said. "Both the owner of a property and the guests are concerned with a substantial investment. The guest may be paying a very handsome sum of money for a two-week vacation in the owner's home, and the owner may be relying on that income for a variety of things. So unlike a traditional hotel, which would maybe offer a 24-hour cancellation period, homeowners don't typically provide that because the likelihood of rebooking that two weeks within 24 hours is very slim. To address this challenge, travel insurance protects guests from unexpected events that could interrupt, or even cause them to cancel, a trip."

Q. What color of bed linens and towels are best to buy?
A. We buy dark sheets because we like the look of them in our properties. If you go with white sheets and towels, make sure that you have a really good washer or consider using a linen service. White can look dingy quickly.

Q. What happens if my property location isn't served by television cable, cellular phone signal, or wired or wireless internet connections?

A. Find a way to turn those minuses into pluses. In the case of no cable TV, having a nice DVD player and a library of movies or a great stereo set-up might be good substitutes. A lack of cell-phone and internet service is a little tougher to spin. You could offer free land-line phone calls and coupons for local attractions in place of cell reception and internet hook-ups. Just be sure to state that you don't have either wired or wireless internet service in your literature — otherwise travelers will assume that you have it.

Let folks know that their cell phones won't work, and then play up the positive aspect of taking a vacation from ring tones and text messages. One clever owner whom we rented from didn't have internet service at his villa on the beach, but he provided a list of all of the nearby coffee shops that did offer free WiFi, and he included some complimentary coupons.

CHAPTER 4

Where Should I Advertise?

Marketing musts…
Marketing mistakes…
What will this cost me?

By now, you have selected a property, researched the market, and prepared your home for guests. It's time to put the word out: I have a great place to rent for your next vacation or business trip! But who is listening? How can you find them? And, at this point, how much or how little advertising will it take to book paying guests?

If you've never advertised before, putting your money where your mouth is may seem like a huge gamble. Telephone books, websites, newspapers, magazines… which of these offer the most visibility? Advertising costs add up fast, so go with your best bets when starting out. Once you build some momentum, you can branch out as well as eliminate ads that aren't working for you.

When you own a business, offers to promote it come from all directions. You might be bombarded by business-card printers, website packagers, discount coupon advertisers, and six different yellow pages companies. Resist these promotions and think like a traveler again. Far and away, listing websites are the most heavily used by people considering or planning vacation stays in private rental homes. These sites should garner the majority of your attention and advertising dollars.

Online vacation rental sites like HomeAway and FlipKey provide the most comprehensive and far-reaching inventories of short-term property rentals available. While there are certainly advanced advertising and marketing strategies that we'll cover in Volume Two for filling your calendar with additional (and diverse) streams of travelers, your first and best source of business will be the major sites. Online browsing eliminates the waits, displays open booking dates, and offers immediate request services to viewers. These power tools are what you will want to plug in to when you first start advertising.

Getting a promotional plan off the ground takes three elements: 1) choosing the right places to advertise; 2) gearing your listing to your target market; and 3) being ready to respond to guest inquiries. Once in business, ensuring that your advertising scheme is working will depend on your oversight, so you will want to create a way to track the success rate of your ads and promotional venues. We'll get into those details in the coming chapters, but let's talk about what the basic steps are now.

Effective Marketing Tools

Don't think that the venues with the greatest number of competing ads will reduce your chances for bookings — the opposite is true. Car dealerships tend to cluster together to attract the largest number of car buyers, right? Being near their competition increases their pool of qualified buyers, who enjoy the chance to shop around in one convenient area. Travelers also like to have choices, and they like to search for the best deals. Comparison shopping is the way to do that. To reach the top of renters' lists, you will put together the best possible listings in the most effective venues, using evaluative tracking and listing-optimization techniques to stay on top. Start by subscribing to the top vacation rental websites. They've already done a lot of the work for you.

The Major Venues

HomeAway.com and its subsidiary, VRBO.com, have consistently performed the best for me. And no, they haven't paid me for that statement. I've tested most of the options on the market, and these two consistently outperform the others, at least for my target demographic and my properties. The sites are user friendly for both owners and travelers, reasonably priced, and very effective. These two sister sites attract slightly different clienteles, so it is worthwhile to share your advertisements with both of them. Additionally, FlipKey. com, now owned by TripAdvisor, the popular travel review site, is another easy-to-use rental listing website that attracts plenty of traffic and consistently comes in third for me, in both volume of leads (interested parties) and conversion ratio (those who end up inquiring and/or making a reservation). An ad with FlipKey gets exponential exposure on TripAdvisor too. These sites all have similar rate structures and services to owners, and provide more than enough advertising exposure to get your venture off the ground.

For just a few hundred dollars a year, paid by flat subscription or percentage per booking, you get a basic flexible account that lets you change your ad content as many times as you like. You can post your real-time calendar openings, and interested trip planners can use the website to request dates, contact you, and exchange agreements and other paperwork. It's an all-inclusive venue, as opposed to traditional print ads that require legwork on the part of both renter and owner.

These online resources provide value-added services for both parties. For instance, owners can generate and store rental agreements securely. Travelers can buy inexpensive trip insurance that protects their vacation investments from costs associated with booking cancellation and damage caused to rental property. These websites attract large numbers from both sides of the business — owners and renters — numbers that just keep growing every year. In short, it would be difficult to go wrong advertising on any of these three sites, as long as you have a quality listing.

Another online option — less attractive to my experience— is Airbnb.com. Its pricing structure requires no monthly or yearly subscription fee up front, but you must pay a per-booking percentage, as opposed to the other sites' available flat rates. Airbnb's demographic is narrow; the site typically attracts budget-minded 20-somethings who are more likely to book economy apartments by the night than vacation homes by the week. Even less desirable is that you give up control over the reservation process: Airbnb handles it on their end, which might sound good, but which greatly limits your ability to screen and speak with guests before they arrive at your place. This goes against everything I've learned about how to stay safe and profitable in this business, so I don't really consider it a viable advertising option for people who want to make a career of hosting.

I recommend using HomeAway, VRBO, and FlipKey because you can accept unlimited bookings for one price, they attract interested quality renters, and you can use the same advertising components on all three sites. There are many ways to upgrade, but in general, for the subscription fee, among other services, you will get:

- standardized listing templates with fill-in-the-blank forms
- easy access to make ad changes anytime
- search functions that help you optimize your ad's visibility
- live reservation calendar
- rental contract facilitation
- revenue and tax tracking tools
- optional reservation management services
- optional online booking and payment services

Basic Ad Components

Creating your listing using website templates couldn't be easier. The three main components are: photographs/images; descriptive copy; and guest reviews. You won't have any reviews yet, but according to Senior Project Manager Jennifer Gold of FlipKey, you can expect to get formal feedback from about every fourth guest party — and more if you work hard at it. These testimonials will become the lifeblood of your listing. Note that while it is easy to create and post an ad on the listing sites, composing a good ad requires both thought and effort.

To get started, put on your traveler hat again and take a look at the properties listed on the major websites. When you type in a location, on the search results page you will see:

- Thumbnail photo of property
- Headline (Beachside Bungalow with Pool and Balcony)

- Subhead (2 Bedrooms, 2 Bathrooms, Sleeps 5)
- Advanced search options (Greater metro area >> metro area house)
- Number of reviews and average rating (7 Reviews ****)
- Current price ($185-$225 per night)

These are the facts that will hook the customer, which you are role-playing. When you want to know more and click on the property title, you will see a full-sized page that includes a larger photo and link to a photo gallery, plus an in-depth description of the property. This is the "meat" of the advertisement, which includes property amenities and distinguishing characteristics.

As you scroll through the listing, you may find: a bio on the owner or manager; an interactive map of the location (but not the physical address, for security purposes); guest reviews; the availability calendar; year-round pricing grid; notes on payment terms and guest restrictions; an email inquiry form; and telephone contact information. In other words, there is room for everything you want to say about your property and how to get in touch with you — and room for everything a potential guest will want to know before considering a stay.

Now switch to your business cap. In composing your ads, use every available option on the template. Post as many photos and amenities as are allowed. Include the area map. FlipKey COO Jeremy Gall notes that "surprisingly, a lot of owners don't include map details in their listing and that can really cost you in map-based searches, particularly on Trip Advisor." A complete and detailed listing increases your credibility as a host and the desirability of your property. See Chapter Five for more on creating tempting advertisements.

Responding to Requests

A great ad can make your property "famous," but a rental inquiry makes you the star. Posting your listing only sets the stage. When the calls come in, it is time to act. In the short-term rental business, response time directly affects how many inquiries will become reservations. I cannot stress this enough: Responding to rental requests in a timely manner is your most important job. There is no other way to bring renters into your property.

The online experience, while useful to those who are planning vacations, increases people's sense of immediacy. We are all used to one-click shopping, lightning downloads, and real-time chatting. Vacation planners are no longer patient enough to wait for a brochure in the mail or even for a leisurely email or phone response. If they are interested in your property, they want to make contact now.

I spoke with Chief Executive Officer Brian Sharples of HomeAway about the importance of response times. His research shows how quick replies influence booking rates: "We know that if you get back to somebody within 8 hours, you have a 50-percent higher probability of getting that booking than if you get back to them in 24 hours." But there's more to the issue than just increasing rental occupancy.

Brian says that swiftly returning calls and updating calendars about property availability creates trust in the listing site's brand and in you as an owner — and not doing so is harmful. Failing to call folks back or to revise your available dates online decreases traffic not only to your ad, but across the website. According to Brian, some owners get requests for dates that are already booked and just ignore the request instead of being courteous and letting the interested party know about it. "This hurts the marketplace in a big way," he relates, and he reminds owners that they are still competing against hotels, which offer immediate online interaction. "If our owners collectively meet their responsibilities to keep their information up to date and respond to requests, traffic on our sites will triple overnight. Travelers will see that they are as usable as hotel websites, but as it is, they can't always trust the data."

Owners who fail in these obligations to prospective guests think that, because they already have a booking, this practice won't hurt anybody. Brian explains that "if 30 percent of owners have bad calendar data or don't make timely contact, that means that customers will have a bad experience 30 percent of the time. This marketplace will expand dramatically if the data is of high quality," he asserts. That means that pulling your own weight will reap benefits for everyone in the business.

So the way in which you handle your responses and rental availability will — in large part — determine the success of your viewed ads. As you subscribe to vacation rental websites and list your property, I suggest you develop a personal protocol for handling renter inquiries. Set a target response time and see if you can nail it. Equip yourself with whatever you need — cell phone, organizer, laptop, pen and notebook — to reply and to store information about potential guests.

Think about it: You might get a dozen requests on a good day. How will you remember which person belonged to which phone number or email address? How you will you remember whether you returned their calls or messages, and what their reactions were?

You will want to make notes that help you remember and identify individuals, in addition to taking their contact info and requested dates. You'll also want to ask them where they heard about your property and record this information. I add it to a personal database that I created specifically to track how well my advertising investments are paying off. We'll talk more about how you can evaluate your marketing system in the following chapter. Now let's look at how to piggyback on the advertisements that you pay for, in order to expand your marketing reach to the fullest.

Additional Niche Advertising

Just because a promo opportunity is free does not mean that it doesn't work. In addition to paid advertising, you can expend a little effort each week to network in person or online and increase your visibility. Note that these venues take more diligence to utilize, but over time, they may bring in the added bookings that your business needs to stay profitable.

Social Media

Have I mentioned social media? What a great networking tool for people in the social business of hosting! Yes, technically, you are just renting out space to short-term guests. But, as I've said, your personality and hosting style are what set your space apart from so many others. Capitalize on your uniqueness by creating a presence on Facebook. When you move up to hosting a personal website, you can add a blog (I'll discuss these at greater length in Volume Two of this series). These should become ongoing projects, but they are likely to reap growing rewards.

Here's what Christine Anderson, a professional copywriter and vacation-rental advertising consultant, has to say about Facebook: "Used correctly can be a great tool because chances are, your guests are already on Facebook, showing pictures of their vacations to their friends. It's also a good way to keep in touch with guests long after they stay at your rental." Christine finds Facebook more suited to this type of connection than Twitter, but she says that owners have to be prepared to follow through once they create a Facebook page. "The worst thing you could do is start it and then not do anything with it," Christine mentions, "because that implies that you don't have follow-through, you're not on top of things." She suggests updating your page with new photos, a note to followers, or a positive review at least once a week, ideally every few days. This makes you look sharp and your enterprise look busy.

Craigslist

Advertising vacation rentals on Craigslist.com is free, but requires renewal of an existing ad before it expires at 30 days. After

30 days, you can repost it from scratch. In other words, you'll need to constantly update a Craigslist ad if you want continuous coverage.

It's easy to create a Craigslist account and fill out the ad template. You can use photos and text, and include a contact link and phone number. Some owners on a budget use this service exclusively, but minus the calendar and reviews, Craigslist generates more work for you and less satisfaction for those browsing available rentals. Another downside is that hackers and scammers may target your ad with alterations or fake booking requests.

Still, Craigslist offers a way to go after every viable renter, especially those looking for economy rates. It also increases your local visibility, because it's sorted by city and surrounding areas. Folks looking for a short-term rental in their own town (where your property is located) or those seeking owner-run properties might be more inclined to visit Craigslist than one of the big listing sites. If the process is too time consuming for your schedule, you might consider advertising here during the off-season or using it to offer midweek specials.

Community Networking

As you interact with contractors, service people, and merchants in your community, don't be shy. Let them know about your vacation rental. When you get to know them, broach the subject of a mutual referral system. You might recommend their remodeling crew, maintenance service, or restaurant to your property owners' alliance, neighbors, and guests. In exchange, they might be willing to let folks know about your rental.

You can perform this type of marketing online as well, trading links to Facebook or business websites for greater exposure. But take advantage of the personal relationships that you cultivate in connection with your business. You never know when they will pay off. We even get referrals from an owner of a local bike shop.

Here's another example: One day I received a package from a builder who had worked on one of my properties, and in it was a really nice bottle of tequila. A note read, "Thanks for helping me close that deal." I was thrilled, but had no idea what I had done to deserve his gratitude, so I called him and asked. He said he had been working with a couple to design a remodel for their master bedroom and kitchen, but they wouldn't commit to a start date. Did they need to look at more tile samples? More paint colors? No, they said it wasn't those things. It finally came out that they had no idea where they would stay during the remodel. It was too long to impose on friends or family, and a lengthy hotel stay would be too uncomfortable, not to mention inconvenient.

My builder friend remembered that my furnished rental was right in the neighborhood, and he suggested they call me. He said that this referral turned the tables on the deal immediately. The couple went from dreading having the work done to looking forward to a mini-vacation, and they scheduled the job. My friend has now referred several guests to me — which closes deals for him and brings in new renters for me — and ours is becoming a valuable relationship.

Another local bond that is advantageous to cement is the one between you and your rental property's neighbors. The trouble over vacation rentals in Austin started because neighboring homeowners imagined all the problems that people in and out of the places next door might cause. I offer a discounted nightly rate to my neighbors, and many take advantage of it to house relatives and friends who come to town. They become much more accepting of short-term rentals if they can take the opportunity to put up visiting in-laws. Another way to defuse suspicions is to hold an open house centered around a happy hour or buffet to which you can invite the folks next door — or everybody on the block. You can even use the event as an excuse to generate a press release for local publications to gain exposure.

Mistakes to Avoid

It may seem obvious, but operating contrary to the above advice is a recipe for failure, at least when you are starting out and building a reputation. In other words, what you don't do may do your business the most harm:

- Advertising on just one site is not enough exposure to guarantee full occupancy.
- An incomplete ad will be overshadowed by those that offer more details.
- Responding slowly to guest inquiries means that others will likely capture those bookings first.
- A lapsed Facebook page or Craigslist ad can be worse than ineffective — it can detract from your reputation and brand.

So, not being thorough or proactive are two of the biggest marketing mistakes you can make. The other common error — which will cost you a bundle — is composing poor advertisements. Scroll through the listings to see which ones turn you off. They are probably the ones with blurry photographs, sparse information, misspellings, and other structural errors.

We'll talk more about these particular problems and their solutions in Chapter Five. My best advice on avoiding pitfalls as you begin to advertise, however, is to put in continual effort and keep moving forward.

***

You Might Ask...

Q. Are the online listing sites all-inclusive?

A. For the beginner, they really are. They let the owner handle advertising, screening, agreements, reservations, and payment processing online. Some even connect to (optional) services that handle collection and remittance of required occupancy taxes. Explore individual websites to find out which services they provide.

Q. What about print advertising?

A. Many communities have thriving regional newspapers geared toward local advertising. These are usually free to customers and have a potentially wide readership and relatively low ad rates. They might be a better bet than big dailies, which are losing readers to online news sources all the time, and which charge more for advertising. Other possible print venues are specialty magazines that your property might appeal to, like ski and hunting magazines for cabins or writers' magazines for quiet, secluded properties conducive to getting that novel done.

Q. Should I install a separate business telephone line as the contact number in my ads?

A. No; save your money. For security purposes, I strongly recommend Google Voice, a free service that provides a contact number that forwards to any of your existing telephones. If you switch cell carriers or move to a new land line, your Google Voice number will stay the same.

How does it work? You can record a professional greeting, and while the caller holds, the system will try different phone numbers until it either reaches you or takes a voice mail message. Then the message is roughly transcribed and sent to you as both an email to your computer and a text message to your primary phone. This way, you never lose a call about your property, and you always know when calls are specifically regarding the property.

CHAPTER 5

How Can I Stand Out?

Killer photos…
Compelling copywriting…
What's the best presentation?

While you can't start booking guests if you don't make contact, you cannot get those calls or emails unless you get renters' attention with an exceptional ad. By now, you have browsed through the online listings many times. Maybe they all look great to you. Now it is time to reach for your next hat — your marketing cap! We may not all be natural-born promoters, but we do all know what we enjoy when we travel, and that's half the battle.

Your advertisement must reach out to others, not simply remind you of how much you have invested in your vacation property. We have already discussed which amenities and services people want most when booking a place to stay. Your competitors are well versed in this area too. Suppose you have a similar property with equal amenities to one down the block. In order to stand out from the crowd, you must present what you have to offer in a more moving way. How is that done? With pictures, with words, and with the utmost attention to detail. And according to Jen Gold of FlipKey, it all starts with the photos.

"Photos are critical," Jen says. "Just having photos at all is important, but beyond that we find that the size and quality of the photos have a direct correlation to the number of inquiries that a property gets. We also find that captions on photos have a high correlation to number of inquiries. I don't think that's something that many owners are doing, and yet we know from our data that the more good photos with captions you have, the higher the number and quality of inquiries you'll receive."

That's because most viewers scan the most important images and text as they scroll through the websites, narrowing down their property options. "Your goal is to stand out and capture their attention before another listing does," Jen instructs owners. "Research shows that travelers spend an average of about two minutes per listing, but that average is a little misleading. What really happens is that, when people get to the property page, they're very quickly making a decision, usually based on the photos: Is this something they're interested in exploring further or not? If not, they hit the back button, or they do another search. Whereas if it is a property that they are interested in, they're going to spend a lot more than two minutes — we estimate somewhere between five and ten minutes. They'll look at photos and drill down on the map, looking to see where the property is, reading the description, reading the reviews, etc…"

So, while viewers start with the photos, they also rely on your written description to help them in their search. Be honest with yourself: Can you provide great text and images yourself? Whether or not you take decent photographs or write well, these may not be your real areas of expertise — otherwise your career history would probably be different. All of the industry experts with whom I work strongly suggest getting professional help in composing your ads. So do I. This is another investment that will pay for itself in increased rental traffic. I learned the difference between using do-it-yourself and professional photographs in my ads firsthand.

***

I had two properties that were identical—the layout, the decor, the number of bedrooms—but I needed to create separate listings for them. I had one property professionally photographed, but in the interest of time, I decided to take pictures of the other one myself. I uploaded what I thought were similar images to both listings and got very different customer responses. Now, I like to think of myself as a decent photographer. I own a good digital camera, I've studied many online listing photos, and I know how to stage a room to look attractive. Yet, as I offered a choice of lodgings to folks I talked to on the phone, they told me they didn't like one of the properties I had advertised because it looked boxy and less comfortable — and that was the one with my photos on the listing. Yikes!

I had to admit that, when compared to the look of the professionally shot property, they were right. The photographer had used more effective lighting and a wider-angle lens to open up that space. As I sat quietly chewing my humble pie, we brought in a professional photographer. The second ad went from passable to exceptional, and the bookings came rolling in. This was pretty clear proof that going with a pro is worth it, preferably one who specializes in real estate photography.

So let's talk more about how your can evaluate the strengths of your property, draft the text and come up with photo ideas — and then make the ad stand out as much as possible by using expert help. You will also want to create a strategy for reviewing the performance of your ads so you can tweak them to remain eye-grabbing as time goes by.

The Vacation Starts Here

What is a vacation rental ad to the reader? It is an infomercial, yes, with pertinent details like pricing and type of housing couched in persuasive language and images. But first, and foremost, a listing ad is viewers' first glimpse at what their vacation might be. Theirs will primarily be an emotional decision. They will have practical considerations, too, but when all is said and done, how they feel about a place is what will seal the deal. First impressions are usually lasting ones, so what appears at the top of your ad is of the utmost importance. Not just "what," either — how you convey the information is what creates that emotional tie.

Can't I just list the number of bedrooms and let the pictures do the talking? Not even close.

An ad is not a one-way street: It is a dialogue between you, the owner, and your target market, the readers. In fact, professional copywriter and consultant Christine Anderson calls it a conversation. "When I'm writing that first paragraph," she relates, "I really try to think about the person that is going to be reading it and write as if I'm speaking with them."

Good advice. People planning their leisure time do not want to be preached at, they want to feel like they're part of the discussion, whether it is online or not. Engaging them in conversation opens them up to what you have to say. Consider how another person's enthusiasm can sell you on a topic, even if it's something you didn't have a real interest in at first. Maybe they tell you about a dish they cooked or a product they discovered in a way that makes you feel like you must make or buy that thing — or really miss out on something special. Their passion becomes yours.

This human tendency to hop on the bandwagon is a big reason why advertising works. Christine advises pouring your passion for your property into the opening lines of your online rental listing. "That is where you need to capture people's attention and really transmit the spirit of the place, as opposed to just stating the details that you can put elsewhere."

To get the most for your money on the listing sites and from consultants' work, you will want to put forth your best efforts first, realizing that there will always be room for improvement. Start spilling it all out on the page, and let your enthusiasm take over. Write down where your property is located and which attractions are nearby, and describe the flavor of the neighborhood. Then mentally walk through your property and list its positive features, and the amenities that you have included. When you're ready to organize and draft an ad, you can prioritize that information and put it into the most advantageous spot in your listing.

To determine what goes where, think about how people read the listings as they are browsing for possible vacation destinations. The ad formats and search functions on the portal sites are geared toward renters' top priorities. What are they? I asked Leah McGarry of HomeAway to break it down for me.

As the product marketing manager, Leah has spent years analyzing how potential renters browse listings. "We just completed a survey of about 1,400 travelers, and what they are looking for is more information to help them narrow down their choices." I had plenty of questions for Leah: How many sites do they look at? How many properties do they compare? Which information is most important to their decisions?

She found that most renters "shop" at more than one website, and look until they find three to six properties that they consider worthy candidates for their vacation time and money. They scan the results page for properties in their price range first and with the right number of bedrooms and bathrooms, and glance at the main photos to see what grabs them. This process might take seconds. So your rates should be carefully crafted, and your first picture should be intriguing. We've also seen an increased use of filters when searching. To avoid falling out of the consideration list, be sure your amenity list is complete, or your property won't show up in the appropriate filters.

Before even delving into the written descriptions, viewers hit the photo galleries and make their own walk-through of a property. One or two pictures won't cut it — to get a realistic view of the layout, six to eight photos are the minimum. HomeAway's research found that travelers prefer the following shots:

- whole house from the outside
- bedrooms (all of them)
- living area
- kitchen
- bathrooms
- outdoor spaces
- view from the property

This tells you what areas of a home are most inviting to renters in choosing accommodations. The order is surprising until you remember how highly most people — and particularly travelers — value a good night's sleep.

While the pictures are what catch their eyes, it is the text that moves viewers to click on a booking button or request form, or to pick up the phone and call you. When I asked Leah for the single most-important factor in prompting this action — the crucial "conversion" from an ad view to an inquiry — she said it was having full and specific info in your listing. "If you're not sharing enough information," she explained, "travelers might be skeptical. They want vivid descriptions, detailed rates and fees, and as many photos as possible. Take advantage of every single space on that listing. Our recent research also indicates that long paragraphs of text are overwhelming so break them up into smaller ones"

You are sharing information, yes. But, with words and pictures, you are also creating a three-dimensional image of your place, where before there was none. And the tone of the writing, or the way in which you present this vision, is what creates the decisive emotional connection that makes readers say, "Yes! I can definitely imagine myself here having a great time." That is the moment when their vacations begin.

***

Drafting an Ad

In beginning to compose your ad, return to the list of basic ad components in the previous chapter and make up a template for yourself on scratch paper or in a computer file. Take your passion-filled notes and run through them with the needs and desires of your target market in mind.

Let's try a sample draft, using your own residence as the property. You might not have a stellar vacation location or luxury amenities to lure readers, so this will help you learn to punch up the strengths of a place and identify its unique selling point. This is the feature that sets your place apart from everyone else's. It should appear in your headline, which you might write last, after you have fully explored the possibilities. Suppose you have a three-bedroom home, which has a bath attached to the master bedroom and a large yard, in a neighborhood on the outskirts of town. Let's say your road dead-ends not far from a river. It is the off-season, and you have yet to welcome guests or get their feedback.

1. Headline (Split-level Privacy near River Access, Grand Opening!)
    Focusing on privacy and what is nearby sounds better than saying "remote" or "dead end." Turn your lack of reviews or rental history into a bonus just as new stores do with a grand opening.

2. Subhead (3 Bedrooms, 3 Bathrooms, Sleeps 7)
    Suppose you have queen beds in two bedrooms, two twin beds in one, and can add a pull-out sofa sleeper in the den, as well as two full bathrooms upstairs and a half bath downstairs. "Sleeps 7" beats "Sleeps 6." Three bathrooms is an accurate count, and you can mention that one is accessed from the master bedroom and one is a half bath in the body of your ad.

3. Advanced search options (State >> area >> neighborhood)
    List both the general area and the specific neighborhood or suburb of your town to zero in on that local target audience or travelers who know exactly where they want to go.

4. Number of reviews and average rating (0 Reviews)
    No, you should definitely not create your own review! That is against the policy of listing sites. Instead, you might add, "Newly Listed" to a photo caption.

5. Current price ($100 per night)
    In the off-season, you will offer your bottom-line rate, in order to draw the most bookings.

6. Overview (A stone's throw from the Clackamas River Scenic Area, gateway to Mount Hood, our split-level hideaway offers solitude and convenient access to area attractions…)

Be careful. This opening paragraph is where the most mistakes are made. Remember Christine Anderson's advice: Use this initial paragraph to convey your property's unique selling points, not which kitchen utensils or how many bedrooms the house has. The number of bedrooms is already incorporated in the search results page and is suggested by your photos. The kitchen details will be included in the template's amenities section.

Don't just list the facts — describe what those facts mean to your readers. (Downstairs sleeping quarters and bath let larger groups spread out in comfort…)

Add news about the surroundings (Quiet, two-lane country road, home to horses, sheep, and cows. Woods surround the property on two sides, and a front gate offers privacy and security). Now you're getting the picture… and so are your readers!

Go on to fill in the tabs regarding the owner's background, full pricing schedule, and the payment and guest requirements that you have worked out. Spend the remainder of your time on listing every single amenity that would interest a renter, adding descriptive adjectives, if the website template allows. For instance, which of these amenity lists sounds better?

- great beds
- cable TV
- internet hook-up

    or:

- New memory-foam mattresses on queen beds
- Flat-screen TV with 200 cable channels
- Reliable, high-speed wireless internet at no extra charge

Now, select the picture that will appear next to your headline. The very first thing that a prospective renter looks at in your listing, besides the price, is that thumbnail photo of your property. What should it be? It's true that blue swimming pools or beachfront waves are yummy eye candy. But, according to HomeAway's Leah McGarry, when given a choice of photos to select and enlarge, readers put bedrooms first on their lists. This doesn't mean that you absolutely have to lead with a bedroom photo, but it's something to consider.

It makes sense: When you are going to spend the night somewhere — away from home, outside your comfort zone — you want to envision where that will be and how it will feel to be in that environment. You might do dozens of things during your vacation, but roughly one-third of your time will be spent sleeping, according to the National Sleep Foundation. So evaluate your property's photo ops with this primary consideration in mind. And remember to include both interior and exterior shots, to let travelers know that your place is divine inside and out.

In addition to serving up pictures of what most concerns travelers, surprising them can also be an effective attention getter. Leah suggests seeing what other owners in your area are featuring and doing something different. If the majority of ads are featuring exteriors, go indoors. If most of them are showing sunny-day outdoor shots or bright interiors, select a nighttime skyline or romantically lit room or patio to draw the reader in.

The beauty of online listing services is that you can change out the photos — and you can use a lot of them. But make that thumbnail count.

Working with Professionals

Now that you have your details sketched out in a rough draft and an idea of what might photograph well in your home, it's time to seek professional help. Here, again, quality will show and will pay off. Yes, you can use your English-teacher aunt to proof your text and your amateur-photographer uncle to snap some photos… but you can also hire someone to do a better — and more objective — job.

When you interview and hire a copywriter, marketing consultant, or photographer, ask these individuals what they need to have in order for them to do their work. If you're prepped and ready to go when you meet or hand off your draft, you will save money in hourly fees or get a better-organized job at a flat rate. This may mean sharing your detailed notes on property features or a completed rough draft with a writer. Or it may mean having your home professionally cleaned, staged, or landscaped before a photo shoot.

Take your time getting to know the people you might work with before making your selection. When you are satisfied with their skill levels and experience, ask yourself one more thing: Can I put my trust in this person? Answer that question to your satisfaction, and you can both proceed with confidence. Then, no matter how much you enjoy controlling a situation, step back and trust them to do their jobs. You might alter text or seek out more photos from another source later… but you are paying for the service, so you might as well get the professionals' A games.

If you work with an experienced real estate photographer, staging your home might be included in the service. If not, Leah McGarry offers a few basic guidelines. "Make sure there is no clutter," she advises. This may mean removing all but one or two decorative items or stowing kitchen appliances that don't photograph well. "We also say avoid showing people in photos. Travelers want to be able to visualize themselves in vacation rentals; they don't necessarily want to see other people there. A hotel website would never have a person in a hotel room photo."

Additionally, to make a room look more spacious — don't add floor-to-ceiling mirrors. According to home decor channel HGTV, these only look outdated. Instead, you might remove an item or two of furniture. Use color to create focal points. A bright flower bouquet or throw pillows add warmth to a room. If you include bathroom photos, make sure the rooms look like new, and make sure the toilet seat is down! Bleach or recaulk tub and sink seams and reglaze tile surfaces for a brand-new shine. If you want to go all out, you can hire a professional home-staging service before taking your listing photographs.

A Clockwork Marketing Plan

The online listing sites make it easy to subscribe and get your ad out into the rental world. Almost immediately, you can begin to learn how well readers are responding to it. HomeAway has added "Listing Performance" metrics in the owner dashboard that allow you to see exactly how your ad is faring in the search results, compared to others. In the graphic here, you can see that this property currently shows up as number seven out of 850 listings in Austin:

Generally, viewers will click on pages sequentially, so whichever ads are higher up in the search queue will be seen first, giving them an advantage in the bookings race.

Jumping over to the Performance tab, we can see how many page views have occurred and how many of those views have converted to inquiries — that key "conversion" metric:

Recent Activity	Listing Info	Performance	Marketing Tools
Year	Month	Pageviews	Inquiries
2013	March	381	45
	February	1131	90
	January	1363	139
	Totals for 2013	2865	274

Simply having an online ad will probably not be enough to produce the results you're looking for. To return to our car dealer metaphor, you've done the right thing by locating your dealership (your ad) next to all the other dealerships (other properties on a high-traffic rental site). So you've ensured that you are in a high-volume stream of traffic — but now we need to make your listing stand out. According to Brian Sharples, HomeAway's CEO, "Property search capabilities on the sites are very powerful and help users really pinpoint what they are looking for, but most people don't use them." He says that although viewers can narrow their search by number of bedrooms, location, or availability dates, "surprisingly, most people still go with the default search." That will undoubtedly change as travelers become more sophisticated and more and more people begin to use vacation rentals.

But for now it means that in order to ensure your highest probability of success, you need to rank as highly as possible with the search engines on your chosen two or three rental sites. You and your copywriter will implement basic search features into the text of your ad by naming the specific location, type of housing, and popular amenities in certain formats. Rising above the competition on the rental listing site can be done a couple of different ways.

The first and most effect way to improve your search rank with FlipKey, VRBO, and HomeAway, for instance, is to have a complete listing. That means every possible space on the ad template filled out in detail, and the full complement of (professional-quality) photos allowed. At this writing, the maximum image count is 24 at VRBO/HomeAway and unlimited at FlipKey. The number of good-quality reviews also drives ad placement at FlipKey, sister company to review mega-site TripAdvisor. See Chapter Eight to learn how to build your portfolio of customer feedback as you start to host guests.

Another search-engine results booster is to offer optional services that the listing site wants to feature. Capabilities for online booking are increasing, and this service helps to push the amount of traffic that the website itself gets. As Leah McGarry relates, the security and convenience of online booking — as opposed to traditional over-the-phone transactions with owners — "is something that travelers prefer, and we reward listings that offer it. Using this tool is one more thing you can do to influence your position in the search results." On HomeAway that tool is called Reservation Manager. (It's similar to third-party booking programs that offer live calendars and online payment transactions, like VacationRentalDesk.com.) A corollary tool called Online Payments will handle all payment processing, including credit cards and echecks. One distinct advantage of HomeAway's payment processing is that, as an owner, you enjoy the lowest credit-card processing rates available. "We offer what are likely the lowest merchant rates on the planet for a transaction without a credit card being present," says Brian Sharples. "People think we make money from payments but the reality is that we only earn a very small amount to help offset customer service costs - we worked very hard to get rates as low as possible and passed these savings directly to our owners". FlipKey has similar tools for reservation management and online payments. Automating payment collection with both of these systems also means one less step for you to take care of.

Paying to upgrade your listing is another search-optimization option on HomeAway, and one that I recommend if you're committed to driving the highest level of occupancy possible for your property. Some owners may balk at the $1,000 price tag for Platinum subscriptions—the highest level of preference in search results — but in my experience, the increase in bookings is well worth the expense. When just starting out, you might opt for a more modestly priced subscription until you get a feel for the market and the daily management. Then you can upgrade when you're ready for greater guest turnover.

Finally, you will want to plot and track your rate of inquiries and bookings from each ad on your own, apart from any tools that the listing websites offer. Each time you add a picture or change a description, you'll be able to see how that affected the number of calls that you get. Experts advise playing with your rate structure to find a happy medium that draws the most bookings by the most desirable renters. Be sure to fully update this pricing information in your ad before springing it on customers. We'll cover how to use analytics to turbocharge your listings in Volume Two, where we'll look at some of the upcoming assessment tools from the major sites as well as some exciting new third-party options that are just coming on the market.

But in the beginning, your main focus should be on presenting a complete listing, great photos, compelling copy, and competitive pricing. Don't leave your advertising to sink or swim on its own. Use this performance information to continually improve text and photos, to add venues for more exposure, and to rethink whatever is not working as well as it could in your marketing program.

***

You Might Ask...

Q. What about slide shows and videos?
A. If they are high definition and professionally shot, they work,

according to Matthew Kellerman of VacationRentalDesk.com, the online booking service. If you have a website served by VacationRentalDesk.com, you can embed a link to your home-tour video on YouTube.com, which will expand your viewership. The rental listing sites also support video links in ads. Experts advise concentrating on getting really good photographs first and then moving up to video, a topic I'll discuss further in Volume Two of this series.

Q. Can I get more guests with special offers and discounts?

A. You bet—travelers especially love a good deal. The Homeowner information on the listing sites will tell you how to add banners and copy to advertise your special offers. These can range from rate cuts to complimentary champagne, used strategically in the off-season or competitive holiday season to steer more guests your way.

"We're always amazed at how few owners post specials, because they really work!" says Jen Gold of FlipKey. "It's something you have to do on a fairly frequent basis because they're timely specials and they run out, but it's one of the most powerful tools on our site to get more inquiries and more bookings. It's surprising that we don't see special offers more often, but when we do see them they absolutely get more inquiries." This is another key marketing topic that will come up in Volume Two.

Q. Can't I have my friends write reviews of my property?

A. Even if your friends have stayed at your place in the past, reviews that are not generated by verifiable bookings won't be accepted by the listing sites or independent travel websites like TripAdvisor. com. If you're worried about seeing a "0 Reviews" tag on your ad, turn it into a positive. Address the fact that you're new in your headline or home description. Many people love the chance to "get there first." Tell them how hard you will try to please them, and you'll soon have that first review.

CHAPTER 6

What Are My Obligations?

Paying taxes…
Legal considerations…
How can I protect myself?

Dealing with legal responsibilities and paperwork is part of your job — and the best way to protect your ability to do business. Remember the challenge to short-term rentals in Austin that I mentioned? One of the reasons that we were able to overcome opposition is that the property owners in our alliance met their obligations: collecting and remitting hotel taxes, following fair-housing rental guidelines, and, ultimately, complying with city regulations. Most owners do these things because it's the honorable way to conduct business. Doing so also helps keep you out of trouble with tax and law-enforcement authorities.

These topics may seem intimidating at first, but once you learn the rules and compose a system for staying within the guidelines, it will all become second nature. I also use and recommend professional services — some geared specifically to vacation rental management — to stay on top of business obligations. The top listing websites will help you handle the rental agreement contracts that protect you from nonpayment and costs associated with property damages.

Among your concerns in welcoming guests to your property are the laws regarding discrimination, truth in advertising, and income reporting. You are free to screen prospects and bar certain types of people from renting — but not others. Making false claims in your ads is illegal and can lead to costly disputes with guests. And I don't have to tell you that keeping accurate books is critical to a healthy relationship with the Internal Revenue Service. Read on for more advice on these subjects.

Avoiding Customer Complaints

I have already introduced you to the Fair Housing and Americans With Disabilities Act legislation that pertain to the vacation rental industry. Additionally, the Federal Trade Commission holds online and print advertisers to certain legal standards. Some of these boundaries are clear, and some are open to interpretation. You should review the full guidelines online (URLs provided below), and you may wish to discuss them with an attorney before you open up shop. Let's talk a bit more about them now.

More on the Fair Housing Act. Get your guest screening protocol down before the calls start coming in. In a rental situation, you cannot discriminate against people just because they are:

- men or women
- children under 18
- religious practitioners
- of a certain race
- from certain countries
- disabled

However, you can turn down a man because he smokes or a woman who wants to bring her pet panther with her.

To avoid allegations of discriminatory practices, you should not ask people in screening calls about their religion or race. You might have a genuine interest in what country they are from, especially if there is a language barrier or special payment arrangement to deal with, so feel free to ask about that — just don't use the information to deny rental.

Families with children under age 18 cannot be barred from a rental. If your place is not kid friendly, you can let callers know this and let them decide to go elsewhere. But it's better to embrace these renters. They may form a large portion of your guest base. In fact, according to HomeAway's CEO Brian Sharples, 85 percent of the site's customers are families traveling with kids. You don't have to worry about damages caused by children because your rental contract and security deposit (or the renters' damage protection insurance) covers them. We encourage families to rent our properties, and we offer the use of a Pack 'n Play upon request.

At this time, age of adults and sexual orientation are not protected by this law. But think very carefully about excluding people for these reasons. While you might not want to risk damage by a houseful of college-aged renters on spring break—barring gay, lesbian, bisexual, and transgendered people who meet your age requirements could harm your business and affect your reputation. Word gets around, and laws may change. And on the flip side of this consideration, in my experience gays and lesbians are avid travelers and also tend to make referrals. We have always made a point of warmly welcoming the LGBT communities.

Get informed before you solidify your rental policies. Read the full text of the Fair Housing Act at U.S. Department of Housing and Urban Development: http://portal.hud.gov/hudportal/HUD?src=/program_offices/fair_housing_equal_opp/FHLaws/yourrights.

More on the Americans With Disabilities Act. Unless you are building a new home or your property was constructed after 1991, you don't have to meet special accessibility design standards that help people with physical limitations or who use wheelchairs or other medical devices. This means, however, that the available pool of rental homes that are appropriate for folks with disabilities is smaller than for the general public. Note that this creates an opportunity for property owners: By retrofitting an older property or exceeding the law's accessibility features on newer homes, your place will become more attractive to this sector of travelers.

Age, in addition to medical conditions, can limit mobility. As the percentage of the population over age 65 increases demographically (think baby boomers), accessible accommodations will likely see an increase in renters. Investments in ramps, wide doorways, roll-in showers, doorknob grippers, and other improvements can eventually pay for themselves in added bookings.

Learn more about the Americans With Disabilities Act by reading the full text at U.S. Department of Justice: http://www.ada.gov/2010ADAstandards_index.htm. Keep your eyes open for updates on the site, as requirements may change. Or contact the Americans With Disabilities Information Line to learn which rules apply to your property at: http://www.ada.gov/infoline.htm.

Advertising Claims

By law, the statements that you make in advertisements "must be truthful, cannot be deceptive or unfair, and must be evidence-based (Title 16, Code of Federal Regulations)." This includes the photographs that you post on your rental listing: 'Photoshopping' presents an interesting challenge. Yes you can make a blue sky with more blue, but you can't drop in a better vista, or cut and paste out elements that you don't like.

Writing truthful ad copy is easy. Don't exaggerate. Report the actual number of bedrooms, the actual square footage, and the actual amenities that you have in place—not what you wish or plan to have. Your entire online listing comes into play under trade laws, however. Pay special attention to accurately conveying your rates and additional fees: Hidden charges can be considered deceptive.

Several laws governed by the Federal Trade Commission may apply to you, including those regarding: endorsements and testimonials (read, "guest reviews"); online advertising; environmental claims (if you promote a "green" property); and basic truthfulness in advertisements. Check out the FTC's Advertising and Marketing page for details before your rental listing goes live: http://business.ftc.gov/advertising-and-marketing.

Drafting Rental Agreements

Most people use the boiler plate contracts provided by the listing services as a starting point, but it's important to determine whether their provisions are right for your property. You'll still need your own rental agreement for bookings that you get from other sources, such as word-of-mouth referral or a personal website, if you build one. You can purchase basic legal forms online from websites such as Legalzoom.

com. But for the greatest financial and liability protection, I suggest that you use strategic wording and have an attorney review your final draft.

Some attorneys suggest not using the terms "rental" or "lease" on your agreement document but instead hiring a lawyer to create a license agreement. This best protects your property in a number of ways, which is why this language is used in the hotel sector. When you stay at a hotel, you sign — whether you realize it or not — a license to stay inside those four walls. It's not a lease. It doesn't convey unrestricted rights to inhabit the property.

Consider what the words rent and lease imply, legally. A long-term lease on a home for rent is designed to protect tenants in the event of a landlord attempting to break the contract. It gives them the right to live on that property. If the landlord wants them to leave, it gives them a set amount of time — often 30 days — to find another place to live. In effect, it becomes their house for the period of the lease plus the required month's notice if they have to move.

The difference between a license and a lease becomes clear when you need to evict a problem or nonpaying inhabitant. With a license, if the guests don't pay the nightly bill, the proprietor can place their stuff in the hallway or out on the street. At a hotel, that's perfectly legal. And that's a protection that vacation-rental property owners can take advantage of. The terms rent and lease imply that the inhabitants are tenants, who have much broader property-access rights than those granted by a short-term license. A license agreement is more limiting: It allows the right to inhabit a furnished space for a finite period of time, after which property owners can exercise their right to forcibly remove trespassers.

If you get into a court dispute, the right wording in your contract may make all the difference. Leases are usually associated with unfurnished dwellings, while licenses are typically used in relation to furnished spaces, as in hotel rooms. Calling your rental agreement a license can also help you come out ahead tax-wise. Let's look more closely at that topic.

Paying Your Taxes

You can declare your income from vacation rentals as strictly property related or as a separate business-operation income. For instance, taking a payment for a week's stay in a private residence is different from taking a payment for a hosted week's stay in which you share the property and provide a service, such as making breakfast, to your guests. The first instance would be a distinct short-term rental; the latter would be considered a bed-and-breakfast arrangement. What's the difference? Rental income is taxed as passive income, while running a B and B is taxed as service-based self-employment at a higher rate.

Certified Public Accountant Stephanie Ball says this distinction is very important to your tax burden. "I advise my clients to specify that they are selling space and time, not services rendered. Keep the lines completely clean and there should be no problem showing that the rental income is for passive activities only." One way to underscore this division is by providing a one-time cleaning fee — for which they are charged, in addition to the base price—after guests leave, rather than performing nightly cleaning and building it into the nightly rate.

In addition to avoiding service-based revenues, you need to keep a tight rein on your spending. According to Stephanie, you can't deduct losses if your adjusted gross income is over $150,000. That means that you need to be able to pay for your house expenses — especially for furnishings — out of your profits. You may need to recognize and step back from your emotions at this point, to achieve that kind of restraint.

"One of the biggest mistakes I see," says Stephanie, "is that people spend too much money and generate big losses in the beginning. Some feel that they're making a statement about themselves, and they spend too much because they feel it's personal, that the property somehow represents them. A client of mine was piling up expenses that she wasn't able to write off on her tax return, and I said, 'You need to quit buying more furniture, more towels, more beds, etc. The place is nice enough; just make some money." Then you can go to Pottery Barn and buy that mirror or those lamps that you wanted. Stephanie suggests tracking your income and expenses via QuickBooks or similar software programs.

In addition to managing your personal taxes, as I touched on earlier in the book, you will need to collect and remit some form of hotel, or room, tax. You can learn about the regulations in your area by checking with the local tax authorities. Because the tax laws change, and because I want there to be absolutely no questions about my compliance, I get professional help from HotSpot Tax Services, which provides month-to-month tax management and consultation specifically for vacation-rental property owners. I'm not paid to endorse the company; it's an affordable service that gives me peace of mind, so I like to share that with other proprietors.

Rob Stephens, owner of HotSpot Tax Services, calls the hotel occupancy tax a sales tax on gross receipts, not an income tax. That makes handling this money additional legal evidence of your role in the business. "It's very clear that the guest is the one paying the tax," Rob says. He notes that, although the regulations vary from state to state, "a very common stipulation is that the tax has to be separately stated in the bill. You, as the operator, are simply collecting it and paying it to the state and city at the appropriate time."

Unraveling the overlapping jurisdictions for hotel taxes can be confusing. Visit your state's and city's official websites to find their tax rules for short-term rentals, or ask your tax preparer if she has this information. Because the vacation rental industry is relatively young, some professionals might not be well versed in its intricacies. I like HotSpot because they deal with the tax laws in every state as they apply to rental property owners. They handle the burden of filling out the right forms for you and applying for any required licenses or permits. Then, for a very reasonable monthly fee, they check your revenue, file your monthly or quarterly returns, and remit the money to the correct agencies. Best of all, if you're a paying customer, they guarantee that your tax collection and remittances will be in compliance, as long as you have supplied them with accurate reporting.

Alternatively, you can look into the tax assistance that your listing websites offer. It's worth noting that HotSpot is the tax-compliance service of choice for HomeAway. The company has an interest in making sure that owners pay occupancy taxes, so they are making it easier to do so. New products that support owners in their business management are being unveiled all the time.

Keeping Licenses Current

When you research your local property-rental regulations, you will find out whether you need to hold a business license and any extra certification. Obviously, you'll want to keep these privileges current by renewing them before they expire. Be sure to include the dates in your business calendar. If you subscribe to HotSpot for tax help, they may perform this service for you.

Share the rest of your questions on tax, legal, and license issues with the folks in your owners' alliance or an online forum. Don't act purely on secondhand advice, but take the opportunity to learn how others are solving their problems and get referrals to trusted professionals. Before long, you'll have mastered the whole system, and you'll sleep better knowing that you're on the right side of the law.

Insuring Your Property

Many owners mistakenly assume that their existing coverage will be sufficient to insure a property that is used for short-term rentals. In some cases, this may be true, but there are enough exceptions that I strongly encourage you to review your policy with your provider. As this market matures, some insurance companies are beginning to offer products tailored to the needs of vacation rental owners. I recently switched my policies to CBIZ, one of the larger business insurance providers in the United States, to gain coverage explicitly designed for vacation rental properties. It's important to note that language and legal guidelines that pertain to insurance differ from those used by tax authorities.

I spoke with Scott Wolf, president of CBIZ Insurance Property and Casualty Division, to learn more about the specific coverage needs in our industry. "In the world of insurance," Scott said, "there are two major categories: homeowner's insurance and commercial insurance. As a vacation rental owner, you need to ensure that you have a commercial insurance policy. Prior to converting a home or second house into a vacation rental, most people insure under a homeowner's policy, which has specific exclusions. For example, there is no liability coverage if there is a business operation in place. When you accept money from someone to rent your property, you're engaging in business, so the homeowner's policy doesn't cover you for your largest exposure, which is liability.

"Liability is where the guest or the renter would bring a suit against you for injuries sustained at the vacation rental — for example if they fell down the steps and want to seek a demand from you. Another major, and potentially costly, misconception is that another type of policy, called a dwelling policy, provides that protection. Dwelling policies are for non-owner-occupied buildings, but they're for long-term rentals. The insurance world has made a clear distinction between long-term and short-term rentals. Short-term are considered businesses, so you have to have a commercial policy to have coverage." That's the opposite of how the IRS defines the type of vacation rental income we are talking about. The good news is that commercial policies don't cost much more than those for private homeowners.

Another plus, and the main reason that I switched to this type of commercial policy, is the coverage provided for lost income—which is not the same thing as lost rent, by the way. Scott clarified that "dwelling policies cover 'loss of rent', not 'loss of business income.' The definition of 'loss of rent' is whatever the market value is for rental income in your area. So if your vacation rental burned to the ground and you had a dwelling policy that had a 'loss of rent' coverage, the adjuster would say, 'Well, the average rental income for a three-bedroom house in your area on a long-term basis is $1,200 per month, and that is what we are going to pay.' We recognize that you may rent your place out for $1,500 per week, and $5,000 per week during special events. So our commercial policies will cover you for loss of income based on historical data, and will even calculate if your rental rates had been increasing. It's just a world of difference in terms of business protection, for what is typically the same or only slightly more cost."

Security Deposit or Trip Insurance?

Once you sort out your general property insurance, it's time to think about costs associated with broken windows, stained upholstery, or other havoc caused by your guests. Most of the time, damage is accidental, not intentional or due to willful negligence. This is where security deposits or damage protection programs come in to benefit both guests and owners.

Traditionally, in any rental situation, the agreement contains a clause regarding who is responsible for covering damages and where that money will come from. The security deposit — in the form of a check, cash, or a hold on a credit-card amount — protects owners from paying to address damages up to a certain sum. It also covers expenses associated with security and climate control, such as lost keys or open doors, and lost revenue in case the premises are not vacated at the agreed time.

Here is a sample from my rental agreement regarding the security deposit:

A damage/reservation deposit of $200 is required. This must be received upon booking the reservation. The deposit automatically converts to a security/damage deposit upon arrival. The deposit is NOT applied toward rent; however, it is fully refundable within (14) days of departure, provided the following provisions are met.

a. No damage is done to unit or its contents beyond normal wear and tear.
b. No charges are incurred due to smoking, additional guests, or undeclared pets.
c. All debris, rubbish, and discards are placed in the trash can and soiled dishes are placed in the dishwasher.
d. Any property keys (laundry room) are in place, on the key rack.
e. All windows and doors are left locked.
f. The thermostat is set according to check-out procedures.
g. No linens are lost or damaged.
h. No artwork is lost, stolen, or damaged.
i. No early check-in or late check-out unless agreed upon.
j. The renter is not evicted by the owner (or representative of the owner), or by the local law enforcement.

Deposits aren't foolproof, though. Extreme damage might exceed the sum you collected in advance. Many owners mistakenly think that having customer credit-card information means they don't need to collect a damage deposit because they can collect on the credit card. That's a gamble. Even if you hold a credit-card amount and do have to put it toward expenses, guests can easily dispute the transaction, and without their signatures you will have a hard time winning in a tussle with the credit agency. George Meshkov of CSA Travel Protection (CSA), a private insurance company that is also a HomeAway partner, suggests avoiding such disagreements. "Owners lose nearly every time on those [claims]. Once in a while VISA is going to side with the owner, but they are in it to protect the guest." He encourages owners to get more, not less, protection. "We see, in some cases, owners will both collect a security deposit and request that the guest purchase a damage protection plan as well."

This increasingly popular supplement or alternative to a security deposit is an inexpensive damage-protection insurance policy that travelers can purchase to cover breakage and other possibilities. Most rental listing sites and some private insurance companies, such as CSA, now offer them. Rather than holding a large refundable sum, this type of trip coverage charges a small nonrefundable fee, which purchases the insurance. In the event of an incident, the insurance company compensates the Guest or if the Guest requests the property owner can be paid directly. Many travelers prefer to pay a nominal sum and then forget about it, rather than waiting the required period for a refund.

I talked with George about the benefits of damage protection coverage over security deposits. Renters can buy these policies at a fraction of typical security deposit rates, which George says pays off for owners as well as guests. It relieves proprietors of collecting, holding, and refunding money in most transactions — costly damage is the exception rather than the norm. The policies also help the owners and guests relationship by providing a financial buffer in the event of accidently broken property.

George describes how damage protection changes the economics of travel for the guest. He explains, "If people book rental homes that cost $5,000 with a security deposit of $1,500, all of a sudden they have a $6,500 bill to pay, in many cases months before ever arriving at the property. If instead guests are offered a $49 solution to insure up to $1,500 in damage, that extra money is now available to put toward the trip." This removes one obstacle in renting a vacation home and makes life easier for both guest and host.

The other popular travel insurance option, available from CSA as well as other vendors, is cancellation protection. While damage protection insurance shields owner and guest from paying to fix or replace damaged rental property or contents, cancellation coverage protects your income and guests' investments in their vacations. The policy pays rental cancellation fees in the event of cancelled flights, or something out of the owner's control — like the property becoming unavailable due to an accident, Illness, damage, or another cause.

Depending on the coverages that are included, comprehensive travel protection policies typically cost between 4 percent and 8 percent of the total lodging cost. George says that since HomeAway started offering CSA insurance products, customer demand has grown substantially every month.

What about little glitches that aren't subject to purchased coverage? Some infractions are too small to argue over but can impact your property or threaten repeat bookings. A guest might break a coffee mug and forget to say anything about it, and your next large party is short a mug at breakfast. Or a light bulb goes out, and your next guest is an avid reader. Rather than including these little things in my contractual agreement with renters, we address them as part of our management system. Our renters' handbook asks folks to help us inventory small items that are used, lost, or broken. That way, they know that we care about whether they need anything replaced, and we can make the next renters happy as well.

Now that you and your guests are set with peace-of-mind solutions, here's my next question: Can you multitask? See the following chapter for tips on how to juggle the daily duties that go along with vacation property ownership.

***

You Might Ask...

Q. How should I address damage by a guest?

A. First decide how serious the matter is. If it's something you want to pursue to recoup repair costs, photograph the damage and locate a purchase receipt, if you have one. If not, find out how much it will cost you to repair or replace the broken lamp, stained sofa, or other item. Then call or email whoever paid the rental bill and: State the damage; quote your damage and security-deposit rule from your payment terms; and explain that you will refund the deposit minus your replacement or repair cost.

If your guests purchased a damage protection policy instead, and if it appears that something broke accidentally, then you might not even have to mention it to the renters. You can deal directly with the insurance claims department. On the other hand, evidence of a party or deliberate misuse of an item might at least warrant a note to the guests acknowledging the damage — or a note to yourself not to rent to those folks again.

Q. How should I handle customer complaints that result in refund requests?

A. Your payment terms should be very explicit regarding refunds in the event of damage, cancellations, or shortened stays. Your screening process and listing ad should let guests know what to expect of your property. If they simply don't like the place as well as they supposed or if they considered your supplies inadequate (and you don't), you can give them an apology but don't have to give them a refund.

A dispute that arises over double booking, denied access due to foreclosure, false advertising claims, or withholding a security deposit may wind up in small-claims court. In that case, you'll need to state your case with an attorney. The major listing sites also offer low-cost travel insurance products that cover all of these scenarios, to refund guests' payments and keep everyone from having to go to court. You might avoid a refund-request situation by encouraging prospective guests to consider buying some type of trip insurance. Send them directly to the listing website's *protection products page.*

Q. What if a complaint leads to a bad review?

A. Bad reviews — deserved or not — happen. Sooner or later, you might drop the ball and make a mistake, or you may encounter one of those travelers who is having a bad day or who simply cannot be pleased, even though you do everything right. The online listing and review sites acknowledge that some bad reviews may be unfounded, so they allow property owners to comment on reviews. This gives you a chance to turn these incidents into customer-service opportunities.

Immediately upon learning of an uncomplimentary review, post a comment that addresses the situation. You don't need to publicly address whether someone was at fault for whatever went wrong, but do apologize for the guest's unhappiness. Whether you failed to provide enough clean towels or a construction crew next door made too much noise, take steps to avoid the problem in the future, if possible — or to alert incoming guests of unavoidable trouble that might affect their stays. Then mention what you did in your comment online. It shows that you're listening and that you care. People will know that you respond to guests' concerns.

Your prompt reply to an online complaint will protect and maybe even strengthen your reputation as a host. Although most owners are very concerned about negative reviews, they don't necessarily affect your listing performance as much as you might think. Jen Gold with FlipKey understands that most viewers take poor ratings with a grain of salt: "Reviews are important, but travelers are pretty savvy to the fact that every property in the world and every restaurant is going to have some one-star reviews and some two-star reviews. It's just a numbers game. A small percentage of people will have a grudge, or didn't have the time of their life, or had one little problem that ruined their whole trip. People train themselves to discount those negative reviews and listen to the majority opinion."

So do take online guest criticism seriously and address it promptly and positively, but realize that a low rating isn't the end of the world. Jen continues, "Especially for negative reviews, I find that having the owner quickly and thoroughly respond can sometimes be more beneficial than having only good reviews. It shows that there is a real person behind this business — someone is addressing any problems and is doing their best to respond."

CHAPTER 7

How Should I Run the House?

Security issues…
Maintenance schedules…
Which supplies do I need?

When the calls and inquiries start coming in, you'll need to be ready to accept guests and turn over the space to new parties while still managing the upkeep in between. So how can you keep your operation tuned, well oiled, and running smoothly? We'll get to housekeeping and guest relations in the next chapter. For now, you'll want to focus on: safety and security; stocks of supplies; and services for ongoing repair and maintenance. Step one: determining how to let people in — and keep people out of — your vacation home.

Keys and Security

Gone are the days when property owners sent physical keys to renters by snail mail or met each and every guest at the doorstep. Just like in real estate sales, those who use keys typically keep them in a combo lock box mounted somewhere at the property. To get in, the code is punched manually, and the box opens to reveal the key. You can change the code in between renters to prevent unscrupulous folks who know about the place from reentering later.

Much better options to my mind, however, are keyless entry systems that can be coded remotely by phone or triggered by built-in algorithms. Say good-bye to lost keys! These electronic systems can be integrated with other remote security features to provide comprehensive protection for your home's contents and guests' personal safety.

In addition to the first-line exterior door locks that you choose, you will need to install deadbolts that can be operated from the inside and good window locks, to deter break-ins. Outdoor security cameras and motion-sensor lights are also highly recommended. Motion-controlled lights can keep strangers from approaching your property, and they make relatively inexpensive and energy-efficient nighttime lighting. Footage recorded by outdoor cameras can tell you whether the trash has been taken out and confirm that no parties were held on the premises. In case of burglary or theft, you will also have a record of anyone or anything going out the door. If you can't afford this type of system yet, put it on your wish list for future investment.

I've recently integrated several security components into my properties for protection, convenience, and peace of mind. Upgrading to "smart" locks, integrated climate control, and remotely controlled lights has been a transformative update for our properties. The keyless-entry sensors interface wirelessly with the rest of the system, providing owner alerts when someone enters or leaves the property — or tries to get in without the proper security code.

The system I use is called Nexia™ Home Intelligence, and it offers a number of easy-to-install components, including: locks, cameras, thermostats, lighting controls, door/window sensors, motions sensors, and small appliance controls — all of which are managed online through a low-cost monthly subscription service. In addition to great security, it is a huge convenience for us. When a tamper alert comes through on a day that guests are checking in, chances are that they wrote their code down incorrectly. The system notifies me instantly, and I can call the guest to help out, often giving their party a pleasant surprise: They have been standing there on the porch for maybe two minutes, and I'm on the line, ready to solve the problem. I can send a remote command over the air to open the door — whether I'm busy at home or on a beach in Mexico — and the guests can get inside immediately. Using Nexia in situations like this produces a high level of customer satisfaction.

The Nexia system works so well that I am always watching to see what the company develops next that can improve my business. I discussed additional modules for my home intelligence system with Mark Schmidt, a business development manager for Ingersoll Rand, makers of Nexia and industry-leading Schlage locks and Trane heating and cooling systems. He mentioned that the Nexia system now includes remote lock, camera, lighting, and thermostat controls, which are all becoming popular with owners of vacation rentals. Temperature monitoring, particularly, is gaining interest fast. As Mark describes, "You can create energy savings schedules for your thermostat. Additionally, you can control energy consumption automatically — if somebody opens the screen door, the system shuts down the air-conditioning unit. On a hot day, what's the first thing people who are staying at a vacation property do? They crank up the air conditioning without a second thought, because they're not paying the bill. Or maybe the A/C wasn't shut off in between guests. Thermostat controls let owners monitor that. They can control the temperature remotely, either when guests are there or when they're not."

The system is very flexible and can be designed to meet the requirements of your property and your situation. Mark and I talked about how the outdoor camera feature saved the owner of a ski-area property from big maintenance bills and travel costs. The owner lived an hour and half away from the rental, and anytime the temperature dipped in the winter, he had to drive out and check on the pipes. He placed a Nexia camera in his crawlspace under the house, and now when it gets extra cold out, he can check the video on his smart phone to see if the pipes have frozen. Thermostat control is surely next on his to-do list. And no, I'm not paid by Nexia (although I would make a great spokesperson). I'm just thrilled with what a difference their service has made in our business. If there is one thing that I would splurge on when launching a vacation rental, it would be this system.

Whichever key system you use, you can program the lock or the lockbox so that each guest party has a unique code that only functions during the time of their stay. With Nexia, I use either a portion of guests' zip codes or phone numbers, for easy recall. You might want to chat with a locksmith or security and home-improvement companies regarding more ways to protect your property from break-ins and other emergencies. These can become liability issues when health and safety are on the line.

In respect to guests' well-being, here are the basic security and safety items you should have:

- smoke detectors
- carbon monoxide detectors
- fire extinguisher (check the charge annually)
- interior deadbolt locks for entry points or braces for sliding doors

I recommend hardwired smoke and CO_2 detectors with battery backups. These are the most advanced models with the best track records, and having these safety items will usually net you an insurance discount. Install a fire extinguisher near the kitchen, and place a sticker or a sign (available at Amazon or Home Depot) pointing out its location nearby.

You should also install inside deadbolts on outer doors, perhaps pairing them with peepholes, and place dowels or other braces on sliding door tracks, to keep them from opening all the way. Make sure you point out these features in your welcome book or home checklist and note that they are meant to keep guests safe from intruders. All of these items will help prevent loss and liability in unfortunate circumstances.

***

In addition to equipping your home for security and safety, you will have to manage the flow of durable and disposable goods for kitchens, bathrooms, laundry rooms, and emergency repairs. Step two in household management: deciding what to have on hand for both staff and guests at your rental property.

Tools and Supplies

You will obviously want to provide linens, paper products, dishwasher and laundry soap, and brooms and dustpans for your rental property. What else do guests need to keep house during their stays? Remember Stephanie Ball's tax advice regarding expenditures: Satisfy needs generously, but don't overbuy. Aside from fixtures, furnishings, and decor, what must you actually provide?

Here's another chance to do it yourself and get answers. Dani and I stay at each of our properties a couple times a year to determine whether everything we — and our guests — need is there and in good working order. This gives us the opportunity to downsize and get rid of unnecessary clutter. It also gives us the chance to experience life's little emergencies. Suppose a light bulb burns out, the power is interrupted, or the toilet overflows? We set guests up for the unexpected with a clear plastic bin full of necessities. We label the contents and ask guests to notify us if they use any of these supplies so we can restock them. Here's a short list of miscellaneous must-haves:

- LED, not incandescent light bulbs
- batteries
- flashlights
- flat-head and Phillips screwdrivers
- duct tape

We also keep a plunger in each bathroom and a broom and mop in a hall closet. A troubleshooting page inserted in our welcome book tells people how to work the thermostat and appliances, replace bulbs and batteries, and flip breaker switches. We don't include devices like hammers or power tools because we don't know how competent guests might be at repairs. But for little things like loose door knobs or pot handles, having a screwdriver lets folks handle small annoyances without having to call us.

Are you always replacing light bulbs at home? Instead of buying traditional incandescent light bulbs, I suggest using LED bulbs, which use fewer watts of power and don't emit heat. This offers significant savings in the long run and also eliminates potential fire hazards. We found out about their superiority over regular light bulbs the hard way: A guest left a fur hat on a lamp, it quickly got too hot, and the lamp caught fire. While LED bulbs cost more per unit up front, they last longer and use less energy than incandescent bulbs. For instance, a major home supply store advertises a 13-watt LED bulb that produces the same light output as a 60-watt regular bulb. Their life spans may be 20 times or greater than old-fashioned light bulbs. Wouldn't it be nice not to have to change bulbs for 15 years?

What else should I buy, and how often? As far as ongoing supplies for guest and staff housekeeping, you will get into a rhythm of what you need and when. You might store bulk items at your residence or in a locked closet or shed on your rental property. Your housekeeper will be responsible for keeping enough guest supplies inside the home, ready for use, and for letting you know when cleaning products are running low.

Err on the generous side regarding disposable supplies like paper products without encouraging waste. You might choose select-a-size paper towels to make it easy to use less, and consider providing laundered cloth napkins instead of throwaway paper ones. Non-disposable necessities like sheets and towels should be inspected by staff when laundering and by yourself periodically, to decide when they must be replaced.

Consider what guests need, and then add a little bit so they never get shortchanged. Don't try to save money on laundry costs by skimping. Stock the kitchen with enough clean dish towels and pot holders, and bathrooms with enough bath and hand towels and wash cloths. Even if you have multiple bathrooms and only singles or couples renting, stock them all. It's only gracious to do so, and makes you look cheap if you don't. Guests don't want to have to hunt down towels when they need them. Many a displeased review concerns this very subject.

You'll need to gauge your volume of linen laundry and be prepared. While it's okay to occasionally make a trip to bring guests additional towels, again, you become suspect if you appear stingy with them. Give your housekeeper enough time to supply clean linens, or use a professional laundry service to stay on top of demand.

***

It is rare that something big breaks down during a guest stay, and Dani and I like to keep it that way. We are also proud of our properties, and performing regular maintenance preserves their beauty and their value. Step three: Let's talk about what type of upkeep you should perform and when.

Routine Maintenance

Obviously, you will want to take care of your biggest business investment—your property. And with the growing number of choices for renters, your home and grounds must wow travelers, or they won't book in the first place or come back for more. If you are like most people, your primary residence gets minimal service until something breaks down. Then you fix it… or you let it go until you feel like fixing it.

That won't do if you wish to avoid expensive and emergency repairs, unhappy guests, and bad reviews. Remember: Most people who rent vacation homes are working off of hotel standards. The better hotels keep things in working order, or at least have the ability to move guests to another room if there is a problem. Unless you have several properties, you probably don't have that luxury.

While you can't plan for every contingency, periodic service will stave off many problems. At my properties, I schedule these major seasonal checks and fixes:

- Monthly: landscaping work as needed; remulch; review bed coverings for wear
- Quarterly: air-conditioning filter replacement; window covering cleaning (drapes, shades, blinds); window cleaning; carpet or rug cleaning
- Annually: HVAC service; irrigation service; water drain line cleaning; A/C drain line cleaning; rain gutter cleaning; fire extinguisher

checks; lawn watering-system checks; hardwood floor deep cleaning; concrete floor waxing or refinishing
- Biannually (every two years): air duct cleaning; refrigerator coil vacuuming

Our properties all have new or near-new home appliances, so we will rely on their warranties if something needs to be fixed. Keeping communication open with guests and housekeepers helps us stay informed: We want to know about glitches like leaky faucets, wobbly chair legs, or weakened bed frames if they arise. Little irritations can become costly plumbing problems. Aging furniture can break and cause injuries and liability issues. Keeping home management and maintenance on a regular schedule, we have more time to do what we love best: getting to know our guests.

***

You Might Ask...

Q. Should I invest in a burglar alarm system?

A. Probably not. There's usually a learning curve associated with operating a burglar alarm system correctly, and short-term renters won't have time to master it. Most communities have strict laws regarding false alarms, and steep fines could end up costing you a bundle. Instead, consider a tamper-alert system that contacts you instead of law enforcement or security guards. Nexia offers door and window sensors that can be integrated with your other home intelligence products to discourage break-ins and to provide peace of mind. This is most practical if you live near your rental property and can swing by to check on the place when you get an alert. If you don't live nearby, you can have your manager or housekeeper alerted.

Q. Where should I buy paper products and supplies?

A. Because we stock multiple properties, running to the store all the time is less than ideal. We order paper towels, toilet tissue, and cleaning supplies through Amazon.com in bulk and have them shipped to us. When you are starting out, though, you might do fine buying your supplies from the grocery store or big-box stores like Costco.

Q. Can I charge customers for carpet cleaning and other maintenance?

A. Your cleaning fee should remain competitive with area pricing (see Chapter Eight for more details.) If you can incorporate part of the cost for quarterly carpet cleaning in your rate without pricing yourself out of the market, fine. If not, build it into your nightly rate during the high season, when travelers are most likely to accept higher rental prices.

CHAPTER 8

How Should I Run My Business?

Management steps…
Handling staff and guests…
Where can I find help?

It's all falling into place… Your house is ready, you're interviewing cleaning staff, and your fledgling enterprise is beginning to look like a long-term adventure into delighting travelers. What will the future look like? At this stage, you can either keep planning and refining your business model — or you can react to situations as they happen. Which road do you think leads to success?

I asked in the first chapter whether you are the organized type. You will need to draw on your inherent Type-A skills to stay on top of the daily nuts and bolts of running your business. From keeping your phone charged to asking your departing guests for reviews, there are many details to remember, but you can use helpful tools so you don't forget any of them. What are you comfortable with? An old-fashioned calendar, a day planner, programs such as Outlook that help you manage email, apps like Things that remind you when to do what? Take your pick, or mix and match. Your colleagues in the rental homeowners' association or the community forums online will have more efficiency-minded suggestions.

With your licenses secured and your ad listing launched, you will start to field inquiries and take reservations. Congratulations! You will soon be hosting a stream of vacationers. Then reality hits. How do I do this? How can I handle that?

Here are two secrets to learning how to run your business: 1) Do your own cleaning, and 2) Read online reviews. At least when you are starting out, I recommend cleaning the place in between guests yourself — in the process, you will learn how you want it done by others. And reviews tell you what real guests like and what turns them off, according to Carol Price, a very successful vacation-rental property owner who garners more five-star reviews than anyone else I know. "If people really want to know how to run a decent place," Carol says, "they should go look at reviews because the answer is in there."

In this chapter I'll touch on the most active aspects of your business. As an involved manager, you will want to know these issues inside and out. As a host, you'll want to practice greeting guests. We're gearing up for the most exciting part of this job: making money doing something that you love.

Automated Bookings

When you first open your doors, I suggest concentrating on running the business using the tools on your advertisement listing website. Subscribing to sites like FlipKey and HomeAway provides availability calendars, your contact info for customer inquiries, rental contract generation, and now reservation management and secure payment portals. You can worry about a personal website and booking management system later, when you are ready to expand — or not, if the listing sites work well enough for you to meet your goals.

Here's how the basic process works:

- A traveler sees your ad and wants to decide between it and a handful of other properties. She clicks on the email contact button or dials the number on your ad listing.
- You answer the phone or dash off an email and answer her questions, which might include: Are these dates available? Do you have a fenced yard? What is the neighborhood like? You can ask her about the number in her party, their reason for traveling, and what type of accommodations she is looking for. She says she'll call or email you back.
- The traveler decides on your place and checks on the availability again. Your online calendar will be up to date. She either clicks on a Book It Now feature, if you have included that in your subscription, or she contacts you again by email or phone to confirm. (You can require a phone call before accepting the booking in order to complete your screening process).
- You accept or decline the reservation, based on how well suited the traveler is to your rental space.

- The website handles the contract and payment transactions.

Sound easy? When you get used to it, it will be.

The listing sites have optional real-time booking as well as credit-card and check payment services available, but not every owner is aware of them. Jen Gold of FlipKey swears by the site's online booking feature, not because her company offers it, but because customers want it. "Travelers prefer online booking and online payments, so use them. You'll set yourself apart from those who don't." Jeff Hurst of HomeAway notes the contribution of these services to higher-quality leads and increased conversions.

The HomeAway product, Jeff says, "lets the traveler generate a real-time quote and even send you a verified payment request for your property. Instead of getting just an email that says, 'I am interested,' you would get an email that says, 'I've seen your quote for South by Southwest [That's one of our biggest tourist draws in Austin.] I understand the minimum standard of pricing, and I have already entered my credit card—give me a call and accept my payment if I check out in your opinion as a guest.'" This removes a step or two for the owner and gives the guest an advantage in the first-come, first-served queue. That really counts during the busy season.

***

My advice for almost everyone in their first year is to take advantage of the great tools that the established listing sites offer. If you're chomping at the bit to expand, though, or just feel more comfortable having complete control over the content of your listing, consider adding a third-party reservation management and payment system like VacationRentalDesk.com. With the added benefit of personalized webpages for your property that you control, this white-label site expands your web presence as it automates booking.

I talked with VacationRentalDesk.com's Matthew Kellerman about how user friendly this online booking service is for new property owners. He says it's simple and fast to get up and going.

"We align an online booking system with a website overnight. Our system is designed to be self-serve, and it's something you can set up very quickly — you don't have to be a computer expert. If you are a computer novice, we have wizards that will help guide you each step of the way, from building your website to uploading your photos, setting your rates and your booking costs, and so forth. That's one of the key benefits of VacationRentalDesk.com: the ease and intuitiveness of our system."

He also mentions that signing up for the company's monthly service includes the website design and hosting — there is no extra charge for that. "They're getting a website built overnight for free, essentially," Matthew says. His advice in using that particular feature includes some of the same things you should already be doing with your main listing ad: Use high-definition, good quality photos and videos to show off your vacation property to its fullest. The online service also integrates with a keyless-entry system, giving you options for consolidating some of your property and business management.

Whether you use only the major listing sites or incorporate a white-label site or a personal website to take bookings, I'll remind you once more: Regardless of where or how you advertise, your rapid response to customer calls and messages is the single most-important factor to closing reservations. I'll go into more detail on how to handle those inquiry and screening phone conversations with prospective guests later in this chapter. Let's move on to the second most-important element of day-to-day business: keeping your property clean and ready for guests to enjoy.

Managing Cleaning Staff

Housekeeping is what keeps your business in motion. Back-to-back bookings leave little time for turnover, so a prompt and thorough cleaning staff is a must. What is prompt, and what is thorough? You can find out by trying it yourself a few times. You don't want to go into the cleaning business — and you don't want to turn your rental income into self-employment — but when you hire housekeepers, you will want to hold them to your standards of cleanliness. What are they? Understanding what your own priorities are will help you hire the right people for the job and will help them get it done well.

Walk through your property room by room, and outdoors if you have yard space. Picture yourself as a guest arriving. A neat and orderly property has much to do with a good first impression. Look around and make a list of what needs to be done on a regular basis to create the right presentation, as well as the big stuff to tackle a couple times a year as the seasons change. Then write down only what you need to do before your first booking. Afterwards, try to do it, with the idea that another set of renters will be coming at your normal check-in time that day.

Laundering linens will show you how much time you need between check-out and check-in to accommodate a houseful of guests. For instance, Dani and I didn't realize that our washing machine and dry cycle were slow until we had to face that fact with more guests coming in. Having that experience of being the cleaners ourselves showed us that we needed a second set of sheets and a second set of towels on the premises in order keep up with the demand at our property.

Housekeepers also act as inspectors. Seeing what the place looks like after guests leave tells you a lot about what was comfortable for them. If they frequently move lamps or rearrange your kitchen, you can address better lighting or easier access to frequently used cookware and utensils. When you hand off clean-up responsibility to a hired housekeeper, you can ask for photos to be sent by phone to assess what shape the place is in after guests check out. You'll also have proof if there are any damages.

Before you engage a service or an individual to clean for you, though, you should form a written checklist that outlines the work you expect to be done, as well as to what degree. In other words, should the dishwasher be unloaded and things simply put away, or should damp items be dried first? Should the toaster be wiped down or cleaned free of crumbs? Should it also be left unplugged?

The little things won't be a big deal until guests find their vacation environment sub-par. Would you want to find lint in the dryer? Hair in the bathtub drain? As you make up your checklist, think with your guests in mind, and also think like a busy house cleaner. What might get glossed over or left undone?

When you are ready to hire help, remember what a great help your cleaning staff will be. Set out to make them happy from moment one: by knowing and being able to articulate clearly what you want done. Consider whether your housekeeper will need to perform tasks outside the normal range of cleaning-only, especially if you live a distance from your property or travel frequently. You might need keys dropped off or a maintenance person met when you can't be there. We like our cleaners to have smart phones so they can take photos if we have questions about the shape of the property, and they can text or email me about any supplies that are needed.

Good social skills are also important for anyone who works on our properties. Housekeepers must be comfortable encountering guests. Every once in a while a guest will disregard your check-out time, and the housekeeper has to be friendly yet firm in saying that it's time to check out so the place can be cleaned — particularly if it's a same-day turnover. And every once in a while guests will show up early. Your housekeeper should be able to put them at ease by offering to keep their bags while they go for a walk, drive, or to a nearby restaurant while the cleaning is completed.

The most important things to Dani and me as owners are that housekeepers are trustworthy and tech savvy, communicate well, and will show up without fail when they are scheduled to work. Beyond that, we need to know that they are going to do a good job. We always tell them to look at the property as if they were guests. In fact, we offer our cleaners free two-night stays during low booking times. This truly allows them to view the home as a guest would, and it conveys our appreciation. We really do have to rely on them to keep our business going.

We have contracted cleaners through a service as well as individuals and teams. Individuals can form a more personal relationship and take more pride in ownership by association with you. They are hired on a 1099 contractual basis, which means that they pay their own income tax. They will not be your employees, but contractors.

The good side to hiring through a service, though, is that you'll have backup when your regular staff gets sick or has an emergency. Professional cleaning services may also offer quality-control checks, which is convenient if you can't always get to your property in between rentals. I suggest checking your area for a service that specializes in vacation rentals. These outfits understand how time-sensitive your business is, and they will select and schedule staff accordingly. In any case, you won't get mixed up in paying employment taxes, as the service covers its staff who are subcontracted to you.

Although you will interview prospects and check their references, you won't know how well workers will meet all of your standards until you put them to the test a few times. Give them the space to work, then monitor the quality of the job. Decide what your "musts" are—attention to detail, flexibility in scheduling and willingness to perform extra tasks—and if they can't meet those needs after a couple tries, move on to find someone who can. Your reputation is at stake, so don't settle for mediocre performance.

You will pass along the cost of cleaning to your renters, just as a landlord would do in a long-term situation. To set your cleaning fee, see what other area owners are charging for housekeeping under their payment terms. Consider your investment in the service, including paying for substitutes when you need them. Don't try to nickel and dime your guests for cleaning in order to make money, though, or you won't be able to compete well for bookings. A recent HomeAway survey found that 64 percent of owners charge guests at cost for cleaning; 12 percent charge less, while 24 percent charge more.

You can use your reminder software to keep track of cleaning schedules and ordering supplies. Once you have your cleaning staff at the ready, it's time to turn your focus on your patrons — the people who will pay your bills.

Interacting With Guests

This is it: The phone rings, or your first email inquiry comes through. You are ready and jumping to respond to your first customers. How should you do it? Enjoying your guests may be a primary objective for you, but you can't get carried away with chitchat. Socializing must coexist with running a solvent business. You will need to be equally capable of getting to know some folks and showing others the door. How you respond to people in various situations will form the foundation of your professional demeanor.

Talk about a balancing act! This is one realm where you will truly learn by doing. None of us can anticipate every scenario. Each case is different, and each day is new. What I can relate to you are some good ways to handle a few of the most common exchanges that will impact your business. Start there, and you'll be on your way to becoming a full-fledged proprietor. Three important areas regarding your interaction with guests are:

- Making first contact/screening
- Welcoming guests onto your property
- Asking guests for reviews after their stay

Let's look at each step.

Your First Contact. If you have a dedicated business number via Google Voice or a cell account, you will know when you get a call that it is a potential or current guest. Answer those calls! You want to create the shortest communication distance between yourself and new prospects, in order to raise your chances of getting or keeping their business. If you aren't able to answer, call back as soon as is humanly possible. Sometimes you'll get an email inquiry with a contact number included. Phone this prospect right away. Calling potential renters is the best way to screen them, and they tend to book more quickly (they like hearing from you!).

When you make contact, you might not need to say much at all. Many folks are passionate about their travel plans and love to talk, so you can easily find out why they are coming to town. Let the conversation flow naturally and see if they answer your questions. If not, ease into your screening process to determine whether you will rent your home to the person on the other end of the line. You want to get a feel for whether they are responsible, honest, or intent on renting a house for illicit purposes or running a payment scam.

Try something like this:

> Hi, Lisa, this is Joel. I received your inquiry on our property in Austin, Texas; it's listing number 54321. Is now a good time to talk? So, you're interested in three nights for four people, right? What brings you to Austin? Have you been here before?

If Lisa says yes, ask if she is familiar with the neighborhood. If not, describe the area and its positive attributes. Listen to her reactions. You want to feel as though Lisa will enjoy staying at your place — this increases the chance of a good review and a repeat booking. If she sounds like she will be a good match, tell her the property is available and describe the booking process. If not, or if she mentions that she wants to use the house for a bachelorette party, either inform her of your strict no-party policy or suggest an alternative venue.

Suppose Lisa increases the number of guests in her group past your maximum, or that you just don't feel comfortable entrusting the house to her. You can decline outright, or if that makes you uncomfortable you can always tell her you have to double-check the calendar because you have some upcoming maintenance scheduled, and you'll get back to her. Or just suggest another place where you think she would be happier.

It may turn out that Lisa is the ideal renter. She wants to make a reservation and make her first payment. Then all you have to do is smile, accept her offer, and get the ball rolling.

Their First Experience

Your guests' first impression of your vacation home and of you as a host can determine the course of your relationship — from ships that pass in the night to a long tradition of return guests who write great reviews and tell all their friends to book from you too. Aside from making the booking process easy and inviting, welcoming your guests onto your property during the first portion of their stay has a lot to do with how they will remember you. It's also an opportunity to make sure that the place is clean and to their liking at the outset. This cuts down on disputes later.

Dani and I have a couple of ways to make newcomers feel at home without having to intrude or hover. We put some things in writing so that guests can read and refer to information at their leisure, and we make sure to make personal contact as well.

First of all, we provide a welcome book. It's one of the first things guests see when they walk through the front door. It's full of information about how to run the house during their stay and also contains insider tips about the neighborhood. Guests love getting suggestions for favorite restaurants and coffee shops, knowing where to shop, and finding out about fun local attractions.

We put a colorful page at the front of the book that says:

"Welcome! Just like you, we love to stay in vacation rentals when we travel. We strive to make your stay as comfortable as possible. If anything needs attention during your stay, please let us know (even if it doesn't bother you). If it's something major, we would like to address it as quickly as possible."

This serves a number of purposes. It puts us on the same footing as guests (we like to stay in vacation rentals too); it humanizes the interaction so they don't feel like they're renting from a corporate conglomerate; and it encourages guests to give us feedback on cleanliness. We've also found that, after reading this, folks feel more comfortable about letting us know if they encountered any broken or malfunctioning furnishings or equipment that need attention. We would rather hear the news while they're still there, so that: a) we can fix it and help them enjoy their stay; and b) they will be less likely to complain about problems in their online reviews.

We also try to either stop by in person or give guests a call shortly after they're scheduled to arrive. This is another area where the Nexia system shines. You can set it up to send you a text alert as soon as the guest uses their code for the first time. Chatting in person or on the phone provides instant appraisal of their first impression and suitability for your property, and you can adjust your vigilance and involvement as host accordingly.

How to Secure a Review

Speaking of getting feedback, your final task in guest relations is to get your renters' reactions in writing — and let's hope they're good ones. Reviews fuel the online selection process for other vacation planners, and they give you huge credibility as an advertiser. The major listing sites work hard to ensure that reviews are verifiable, verbatim entries from guests who have actually stayed at the properties they're writing about. I spoke about this issue with Co-founder and Chief Operating Officer of FlipKey Jeremy Gall, mentioning that many of the owners in our Austin alliance lose sleep over these guest ratings.

Jeremy says vacation planners read online testimonials to help them make important choices on big-ticket items — their vacations. "The research into spending patterns for the average consumer shows that reviews influence all purchasing decisions. I think they're very important. You don't go to the movies unless you've seen what Rotten Tomatoes says about a film. You don't buy a book or anything on Amazon unless you take a look at those reviews." These corroborations build consumer trust, a crucial factor in online commerce. "Are reviews the primary driver of your purchasing decision? Not necessarily," Jeremy admits, "but I do believe they are probably that 'last mile' factor that pushes you over the edge and gives you enough confidence to actually make the purchase, or book a vacation rental."

Still, for the owner who sweats over low ratings, these are not the end of the world. Readers expect some negative input on a property and look more at the average rating. Some vacation planners even see too many excellent reviews as suspect. I talked with Carol Price, a vacation property owner who has one listing with 72 five-star reviews! I asked if anyone ever questioned them, and she said yes: "One lady told me, 'I saw your reviews. How come they're all good? Where's your bad ones?' She felt that I should have a few not-good reviews, so it would seem more realistic." Carol wasn't too worried about that, though.

So, how do you go about getting those five stars? I asked the expert not only how she does it consistently, but why she tries so hard to secure reviews. Expecting Carol to dazzle me with some marketing secrets, I was surprised by her down-to-earth answer.

Carol sees guest ratings as more than an advertising booster — they create a network among renters, she says, and a means to share their joy over a great vacation. Empowering those who stay at rentals to share their experiences complements what owners learn about their guests. "I realized early on that I get to know a lot about the customers: I get their names, their credit card numbers, their contact information, and their family details… but they don't know anything about me. I'm just another house in a bunch of them," Carol told me. She knows how much people love to reminisce about the details of their vacations with friends. "So I reckon if I can get people to talk about me and talk about our properties, then they'll get to know something and can pass that along to other people." Guests get to relive their vacations, and at the same time, the owner's reputation gets a lift.

Carol asks guests to consider writing reviews while they are still on the property. She uses this point of contact to check on the details of their stays. For example, when Carol asked one guest how the vacation was going and for permission to request a review, the woman said, 'Sure," and mentioned that a light bulb was out and that the kitchen was missing a pancake turner. Carol sent an email requesting a review and thanking the guest for the early feedback — she also replaced the light bulb and utensil immediately.

This translates into great customer satisfaction. "I get a lot of people telling me this is the best short-term rental that they've ever been in, and I think it's because they don't have to do anything or think of anything once they get there." Carol shows that by listening to guests' feedback, owners can anticipate, meet, and exceed their needs. To the renters, it seems like magic, but it's really based on being proactive and willing to listen and respond.

Some owners leave signs or postcards with the listing-site URLs in the vacation home encouraging guests to give public feedback. Asking customers to rate your property and post a review with the listing service, however, doesn't mean that they will do so. People get busy. They go home from vacation and have to unpack and go back to work, and the excitement of their time off fades. Here is where Carol shines. She plants the seed of sharing guest experiences while they are in the thick of it, and then follows up assiduously until the reviews roll in. "I tell them up front that they'll get a 10-percent discount on a non-special-event weekend stay for giving me a review. Before they head home, they've already had a chance to think about what they might want to say and to think about coming back. As soon as they agree to that, I send them an email request. A lot of times my guests post their reviews from the airport or on their way home in their cars, because I'm really on it. If they don't write a review within a few days, I send a message saying, 'Did you get the request?'"

Since the renters have already agreed to provide feedback, reminders aren't seen as intrusive or annoying. When your guests are gracious enough to follow through, be sure to thank them—and to take to heart what they have to say. Their comments will help you refine your business model. "If you go back and read through the reviews," Carol noted, "over and over again, people comment on the same things. In our case, it's always the well-stocked kitchen, the well-stocked bedroom, the towels, the sheets, the blankets…" This tells you what is important to travelers and where your investments are well spent.

It's interesting to think that simply hearing about and responding to what guests enjoyed most can lead to vacation rental success. Getting the most for the money that you put into your vacation property will help you keep it in great shape while maximizing your profits. That builds the kind of momentum that will sustain your business in the long term. As you compile a roster of satisfied guests and a system for serving them well, you will also be designing a lifestyle that will carry you into the future — wherever you want to go.

***

You Might Ask…

Q. How can I avoid double booking?

A. If you stick with the listing websites' internal reservation systems and/or a third-party service like VacationRentalDesk.com, the calendars automatically exclude rented dates from viability. You can't go wrong. Using VacationRentalDesk.com, I have never double booked. I always have access to information about guests and their rental agreements, and the service has become the hub of my info management system. We started with this system before HomeAway or FlipKey offered their reservation management systems, but theirs offer the same benefits — the most important being no double bookings.

Q. Do housekeepers need to be bonded and insured?

A. The old saying is true: It's hard to get good help. You might have to make trade-offs regarding bonds and insurance that protect owners from theft or damage by workers. Typically, cleaning services purchase these insurance products for their employees. Individuals whom you hire may or may not carry bonds and insurance.

You will have to decide whether to gamble without them. A longtime housekeeper whose references show no history of theft or illicit activity might be fine without posting a bond to cover losses associated with those types of behavior. If you have good warranties on household appliances that housekeepers use and believe that accidents occasionally happen, you might not require your cleaners to carry damage insurance. It's your call.

Q. Should I keep a guestbook?

A. Yes! I find that guests are more likely to write in a guestbook during their stay or as they are leaving than to bother with an online review at those times. However, once the trip is over and folks get back into their daily routines, encouraging them to post their thoughts on the listing site can be difficult. If they write something lovely in your guestbook, you can type it up yourself and enter it on HomeAway as an "owner submitted review." Or you can enter what they wrote in an email to the authors, asking them to submit it online. This shortens the process for them, and may make all the difference for those who are less comfortable on the computer.

Conclusion

Congratulations! If you've made it this far then hopefully you're well on your way to Vacation Rental Success. Perhaps you've already welcomed your first guests. I hope this book has been useful, and I hope that you've experienced the fun, satisfaction, and fulfilment as a vacation rental owner that Dani and I have with our properties. But it doesn't stop here.

In Volume II, Advanced Concepts, we build on the knowledge we've gained in this book and begin to really maximize every aspect of your vacation rental business. We'll look at tools for anaylzing how well your advertisements are performing. We'll discuss some of the strategic joint ventures and business relationships you can take advantage of to really drive your booking rates through the roof. We'll discuss all of the sources of new business that aren't immediately obvious. In short, we're going to get serious about filling in your calendar.

Look for Vacation Rental Success – Volume II: Advanced Concepts on Amazon, Kindle, and the Apple iBookStore. And don't forget to stop by joelrasmussen.com to get access to the extra chapters and bonuses for this book. Here's to your success!

-Joel Rasmussen

15094207R00081

Made in the USA
San Bernardino, CA
14 September 2014